SOUTHAMPTON
CITY COUNCIL

MORE SOUTHAMPTON CHANGING FACES

JIM BROWN

DB PUBLISHING

First published in Great Britain in 2008 by The Breedon Books Publishing Company Limited
Breedon House, 3 The Parker Centre, Derby, DE21 4SZ

This paperback edition published in Great Britain in 2013 by DB Publishing, an imprint of JMD Media Ltd

ISBN: 978-1-78091-327-8

Printed and bound in the UK by Copytech (UK) Ltd Peterborough

ACKNOWLEDGEMENTS

I am deeply indebted to the following, without whose assistance in either providing access or information, many of the photographs, especially some of the modern ones, could not have been included in this book: Elaine Knight, of Pope Priestley Architects LLP; Paul Wright and Kim Stephens of E.R. Wright and Son; Jennifer Allcott and David Richardson of Orions Point; Jean Underhill; Terry Dyer of Dyer's Boatyard; Ian Abrahams of Bitterne Local History Society; and Paul Tickner and Val Ford of Southampton City Council Civic Centre staff.

Tribute must also be paid to the staff of the City Council in the Archives, Local Collections and Local Studies Library, whose unfailing and cheerful willingness to help was, as always, invaluable. This especially applies to Sue Woolgar, Archives Manager, for her helpful assistance in arranging for this book to be a joint publication with Southampton City Council, thus affording me access to the various city collections. I also thank Joan Holt, my wife Marion, Joanne Smith and Susan Hill (the last two Archives' staff) for their very useful help in proofreading my draft manuscripts.

I would like to acknowledge my appreciation of the many copyright holders who gave permission to reproduce their images, chief among them Mr Harlow, the owner of the Martin collection at the Archives. However, some images were made by companies or individuals who could not be traced. If somebody's copyright has thus been in any way inadvertently infringed, I can only apologise and hope to be excused in the cause of promoting interest in, and the sharing of, our local heritage.

My most grateful thanks must be reserved for Diana Marriott, Archives Conservator at the City Archives. She has spent considerable time seeking out relevant sets of photographs for me to examine and rescanning those chosen to the resolution level required by the printers.

J.W.M. Brown

FOREWORD

Southampton has a rich and diverse heritage of great importance and interest to local people and to those now living across the world who have a connection with the city. The tremendous and event-packed history of this port city has left its mark on the city we see around us today.

This book brings our past and present together in a collection of photographs and draws heavily on the wealth of historical photographs of the city held within the Southampton City Archives and Heritage collections. It is a tribute to all those professional and leisure photographers who have captured inspiring moments through the lens.

Over the last 100 years the City Council has collected over a quarter of a million photographs from a variety of sources to record the ever-changing city around us. The Council has commissioned some, like the World War Two photographic record of damage to every building, or the various slum clearances from the 1920s–1960s. Professional photographic studios have deposited other photographs. There is also a significant and increasing quantity taken by private individuals, which have come either direct or through relatives and friends. We are all indebted to those who have so generously given or loaned their material to the collections.

This book provides a snapshot into this great wealth of material and publishes many photographs for the very first time. It is a fascinating trip down memory lane, with glimpses of Southampton as it used to be and how it has shaped our home of today.

Councillor John M. Hannides
Cabinet Member for Leisure, Culture and Heritage

If your interest in local history has been whetted by this book and you want to go further, the following may be able to help; access arrangements and further information about each can be found on the City Council website **www.southampton.gov.uk**.

Archives, South Block, Civic Centre, tel: 023 8083 2251
Local Studies Library, North Block, Civic Centre, tel: 023 8083 2205
Museums Local Collections, tel: 023 8023 7584

INTRODUCTION

Southampton has experienced many 'changing faces' in its long history, ranging from its early days as the Roman port of Clausentum, to the Anglo-Saxon Hamwic and the Norman town of Hamtun that eventually developed into the modern city of Southampton. In more recent times, changes were brought about when the Victorian slums were eradicated in the early 20th century, when the borough expanded in the 1920s, and, most dramatic of all, when the town suffered severe damage during World War Two. The Luftwaffe's *blitzkreig* destroyed large sections of the town centre as well as causing widespread damage in the outer suburbs, and this took many years to rectify.

Post-war development in the early 1950s brought about what were then new and exciting changes, although many of the buildings were of a temporary nature. Development continued into the 1960s as modern thinking set new standards for both business and domestic buildings, and many surviving pre-war areas were considered to be 'past their sell-by date'. This resulted in such measures as the Hoglands Compulsory Purchase Order of 1956 and the Northam, Shirley and other Clearance Orders of the early 1960s, when complete streets were demolished, with terraced housing often replaced by large multi-storey apartments.

Before these measures were implemented, life for ordinary working people revolved around their work, their local pub, corner shop and post office, the latter three acting as focal meeting points and an important part of the fabric of society. People exchanged views over the garden fences of their small gardens and housewives gossiped while cleaning their front doorsteps and their part of the pavement. Neighbours knew and trusted one another, and they met frequently: in their local public house, while shopping in the corner shop or drawing their pension in the local post office.

All this changed when tower blocks and different types of housing were built, and many individuals became more isolated. Corner shops have been replaced by out-of-town supermarkets, many public houses have vanished and post offices are a fast-disappearing amenity. These changes have continued, in a more piecemeal manner, into the 21st century. This book tries to recapture the former atmosphere by showing now vanished houses, corner shops, public houses and other pre-war buildings. They will hopefully rekindle nostalgic memories or, in some cases, reveal where one's parents or grandparents once lived or socialised.

This has only been possible because the Council made certain that photographs were taken of many streets before they were demolished, to ensure that part of our vanished local heritage can still be seen. Readers with internet access can see many of them on the fascinating website **www.plimsoll.org**, a Port Cities site that features Southampton as the 'Gateway to the World' and gives a search facility to view the many vanished Southampton streets and buildings. Prints of those photographs can be ordered from that website.

I have been fortunate to have been allowed access to the vast collections held by Southampton City Council and hope that this resultant book, a sequel to my *Southampton's Changing Faces*, published by Breedon Books in 2005, will evoke memories of the places where you lived or socialised. Alternatively it will give a glimpse of the living conditions experienced by your ancestors.

Jim Brown, February 2008

Looking west along Central Bridge, built 1882, with storage bays under the arches and the Cattle Market on the left. On the right, at 72 Terminus Terrace, is the Bristol Hotel, on the corner with Richmond Street. Its licence was suspended in 1963 and it was demolished soon after. To its left is A.R. Simmons, Printers.

The scene has now changed dramatically. The large office block on the left is Richmond House, home of the Carnival group of cruise lines, including P&O Cruises, Cunard, P&O Princess, Ocean Village and Swan Hellenic, all scheduled to move to new premises. The tall Mercury Point apartment block is to its right.

The 1846 map shows the building on the left, on the corner of Terminus Terrace and Oxford Street, as the original Railway Hotel. This photograph was taken after 1870, when it was called the London Spirit Stores and Robert Davis had called his adjoining premises, in the centre of the picture, the Railway Hotel.

The London Spirit Stores changed its name to the London Hotel in 1907, when the present building was erected. The Railway Hotel is now private accommodation. The former Flowers Hotel, Jersey & Guernsey Hotel, Hobbs Hotel and the Hotel de Havre (all Temperance hotels) are now shipping offices.

This post-war photograph, looking along Terminus Terrace with St Mary's Church in the background, was taken from the roof of the South Western Hotel. In the foreground are railway wagons of the Terminus Railway Station, and arches under the bridge (used for storage in the old cattle market days) are just visible.

Safety factors now prohibit access to the roof, but this photograph, taken from the top of the internal staircase, shows vast changes. The Terminus Station building is now a casino, modern office blocks have been constructed along Terminus Terrace and pleasant housing now occupies the former railway area.

The South Western Garage, at the junction of Marsh Lane and Terminus Terrace, in 1959. An Esso garage and main Rover and Land Rover dealer, it was on the west side of the Central Station Bridge, opposite the Southampton College of Art buildings, with the pedestrian bridge over the railway to its left.

The South Western Garage petrol station succumbed to the financial pressures of larger outlets and has been replaced by a modern office block. The pedestrian bridge still exists, now serving newly-built massive apartment blocks in Chapel. On the far left are the City Commerce Centre industrial buildings.

Perrin's Motors Ltd, at 17 to 20 Marsh Lane, at the junction with Threefield Lane, was well known in the town as the main dealer for Vauxhall and Bedford vehicles. This view is looking east towards the Central Bridge and Terminus Terrace, with the wall of the Southampton College of Art just out of sight on the left.

The massive tower block offices of Dukes Keep now soar above the otherwise empty site of the former Perrin's Motors showrooms and service centre. The new office block along Threefield Lane is appropriately called Threefield House, occupied by Jardine Lloyd Thompson UK Ltd and the Equity Insurance Group.

Threefield Lane in 1958, looking towards Marsh Lane, with the Methodist Central Hall in the background. On the left, at the junction with Chandos Street, is the Anchor and Hope public house, which dates back to 1875. On the right, on the corner with Richmond Street, is Kemps Hotel, dating back to the early 1860s.

The Anchor and Hope is still there, but in a dilapidated condition, and the former large block of flats beyond it has been rebuilt. Kemps Hotel was demolished in 1970 and the entire block on that side, formerly the warehouse of Burgess, Webb and Squire Ltd and Burrows Transport, has been replaced by offices.

George Rogers, cycle dealer, at No. 52 Threefield Lane in early 1956, adjacent to the Fireman's Arms at 20 Chandos Street. In 1869 the pub was known as the Freemason's Arms, but it changed to the Fireman's Arms in the 1880s. In July 1903 the landlord was fined 10s for selling intoxicating liquor outside normal hours.

The licence for the Fireman's Arms was suspended in June 1956 and it was demolished shortly afterwards. The spot is now occupied by the rear of a block of council flats, built in the late 1950s on the site of the former cycle dealer and adjacent terraced houses.

Canute Road *c.*1895, with hansom cabs patiently waiting for customers. The hotel in the background was built adjoining the Terminus Railway Station in 1867, after Southampton became a main passenger port. It was taken over and renamed 'South Western' by the London & South Western Railway Company in 1871.

The South Western Hotel was requisitioned by the Navy in 1940 and given the title HMS *Shrapnel*. The collaborator Lord Haw Haw broadcast it as having been sunk! It never reverted to being a hotel and is now a luxury apartment block. The Ship Tavern, badly damaged in the Blitz, closed in 1933 and became a café.

The north side of Canute Road, near the junction with Royal Crescent Road *c.*1990. On the left, next to Sgt Pepper's Wine Bar, is the popular Southampton Dockworkers' Social Club, conveniently accessible from the docks. On the right, next to the newsagent's, is the Canute Castle Hotel, which dates back to the early 1850s.

The National Dock Labour Board Scheme, which governed dock workers' employment, was abolished in 1989, and Associated British Ports later replaced their workforce with independent contractors. The redundant social club was ruined in a fire, and new apartments have been built on the site.

Formed in 1836, the Southampton Dock Company was taken over by the L & SW Railway Co. in 1892. Docks administration had been carried on from a nearby building from 1872 until this office block in Canute Road was built in 1962, for what had, in 1953, become the British Transport Docks Board (BTDB).

BTDB became Associated British Ports (ABP) in 1982, but by 1990 it had ceased to retain its own dock labour force and no longer needed such a large administration building. The block was replaced by these luxury apartments when ABP relocated to a new purpose-built 'Ocean Gate' office block near 45 Berth.

Havelock Chambers, on the corner of Queen's Terrace and Latimer Street, was devoted to shipping and other associated organisations, including the American Express Co., the National Union of Seamen, Keller, Bryant & Co. and Bell Hemsley Ltd. W. Bates & Co., chemists, can be seen on the corner of Oxford Street.

Havelock House is no longer a hive of industry dealing with various shipping matters. It has only a few tenants and is now up for sale. The former derelict plot behind it in Latimer Street is now a modern office block and W. Bates, chemists, is now the Prezzo Restaurant, with Italian-style menus.

Looking west along Queen's Terrace in the 1980s, towards Orchard Place, one can see, from left to right: the Surrey Hotel on the corner of Orchard Place; the Alexandra House shipping offices at 10/11 Queen's Terrace; and the edge of the Missions to Seamen's Church and Flying Angel Club on the far right.

The entire block has been redeveloped. The Norwich Union offices, at 1 Queen's Terrace, have been built on the site of the Surrey Hotel, which closed in 1988; a rebuilt Alexander House still houses companies with shipping interests; and the Missions to Seamen's building is now the Southampton Seafarers' Centre.

Queen's Park, so named because nearby God's House and much of the area was granted to the newly formed Queen's College, Oxford by Edward III in 1344. The memorial of four marble columns on a granite block, surmounted by a cross, is a tribute to General 'Chinese' Gordon, who was killed in Khartoum in 1885.

The memorial is still in excellent condition, but the former Georgian terrace, including the Jellicoe Memorial Sailors' Hostel, has been replaced by massive blocks of luxury apartments with penthouses overlooking the Solent. On the left, partially obscured, are God's House Tower and the Old Bowling Green.

A very early sketch of God's House Tower, which was constructed in about 1430. It served as the residence of the town's gunner and also as a magazine. It is the earliest example of a purpose-built residential gun-tower in England, and it provided artillery protection to the south-east corner of the town.

It is not possible to take a photograph from the same position as that of the engraver, but modern developments, which are continuing, can be seen. Beyond the wall on the far right lies Southampton's Old Bowling Green, said to be the oldest in the world, where the game has been played continuously since 1299.

Wartime damage sustained by the Edwin Jones & Co. Furnishing Workrooms at the Town Quay. They advertised themselves as specialists in upholstery, polishing, loose covers, curtains, carpets and all renovations. Next door is the Platform Tavern, opened in 1872 and badly damaged in November 1940.

The demolished section of the Furnishing Workrooms was redeveloped as an attractive office block, and the remainder is now called Eastgate House. The Platform Tavern was completely rebuilt, since only the shell remained after bombing, and it reopened in March 1954. It had a further refurbishment in 1988.

The original Sun Hotel, at the bottom of the High Street and near the Town Quay, dated back to at least 1873 and was destroyed in the Blitz of 1940. It was replaced by this 'temporary' wooden shack, and for nearly 50 years it was the only survivor of the many temporary pubs erected during and just after the war.

The public house was said to have been built by thirsty Canadians just before D-Day in 1944, but it closed in June 1990. It was boarded up and left vacant until it was demolished in 1994. A modern office block now stands on the site and the former large GPO office block is in the throes of conversion to apartments.

The imposing Castle Hotel, at 85 High Street, was on the corner of Porters Lane and dated back to the 1820s. This photograph was taken *c.*1870, when Thomas Mead was the licensee. The hotel closed in the late 1880s and was used as offices until it was badly damaged in World War Two.

The site now forms part of a group of mediaeval ruins that have been preserved at the bottom of the High Street. The castle walls have been revealed now that the false front of the Castle Hotel has been taken down. The former Corn Exchange building, left of the Castle Hotel, is now the La Regata Restaurant and Tapas Bar.

A 1941 view of a building in Albion Terrace that survived the Blitz, at the top of the well-known 'Forty Steps' leading to Western Esplanade. The 1845–46 town map shows a Female Orphan Asylum on the site. A car park has replaced the properties, which were mainly occupied by solicitors.

The Waterman's Arms, High Street, on the corner of Porters Lane, shown in 1910. Adjoining it is the Vine Hotel, which dates back to at least 1772, when in February that year it became the first meeting place of Southampton's Freemasons. Flattened in the war, the area is now Quilter's Archaeological Site.

The tall *Mayflower* memorial column was unveiled on Western Esplanade on 15 August 1913, the anniversary of the day the Pilgrim Fathers embarked from the nearby West Quay in 1620. On the right is the Royal Pier, opened in 1833 by the Duchess of Kent, accompanied by her daughter, Princess Victoria.

The nine-pounder guns and other cannon, some of which were relics of the siege of Sebastopol, presented by the War Office in 1857, were removed during World War Two and the metal used as part of the war effort. The Royal Pier was severely damaged by fire in 1988 and has never reverted to its former use.

One of the oldest streets in the city, possibly 14th century, Cuckoo Lane looks towards the Tudor Merchants Hall and the Westgate Guardroom in 1920. The hall used to stand in St Michael's Square as part of the fish market but was moved to near Westgate in 1634. The spire of St Michael's Church can be seen on the right.

Tudor Merchants Hall and Westgate on the left can now be seen more clearly and the spire of St Michael's is obscured by a modern apartment block. The old houses in Cuckoo Lane have been demolished to give a clearer view of Westgate Street and a large block of flats is on the site of the ancient Southampton Castle.

A *c.*1910 view of the lower High Street, looking north. On the right is Barling & Son, wholesale grocers, followed by the Chamber of Commerce and Hartley College (the forerunner of Southampton University). On the left is R. Brown, stationer, T. Rudd, fine art dealer, and Gricourt et Fils, wholesale wine merchants.

The Goldsmith Court block of apartments has been built on the site of the former shops and Hartley College on the right, and similar blocks are under construction on the left. The church spire seen in the earlier photograph was that of St Lawrence, built *c.*1760 and demolished in 1925 as redundant.

Looking south along the High Street from the junction with Bernard Street, *c.*1900. Smith & Lewis, drapers, are at Nos 40–41, on the left corner, and next door is the Nag's Head public house, dating from around 1740. William Crambrook, silversmith and jeweller, is on the opposite corner with St Michael's Street.

The Blitz of World War Two destroyed much of the east side of the High Street, including the Nag's Head. It was rebuilt and reopened in November 1957 and was later called Fiddlers. It then became a wine store for many years but was empty when this photograph was taken in 2006. Crambrooks is now a futon store.

Bridge Street, *c.*1900. On the left, towards the High Street, is Sanby & Co., ironmongers; the Public Benefit Boot Co.; Charles Smith, hairdresser; and the Greyhound public house. On the right, next to Holy Rood Church, is William Jenvey, wine and spirit merchant. The National Westminster Bank is in the background.

Holy Rood Church lost its spire during the 1940 Blitz and is now a Merchant Navy Memorial site. Lorry parking and Geest Bananas Ltd now occupy the south side of the renamed Bernard Street and a large Job Centre Plus has replaced William Jenvey's store. The spire of St Michael's Church can still be seen.

A pre-war view looking up the High Street from near the junction with Bernard Street. The Georgian Dolphin Hotel is on the right and beyond it can just be seen the faint outline of St Lawrence's Church. Southampton's electric tram service commenced in 1900 and the open-top tram is en route to the docks.

All the fine premises on the west of the High Street were completely destroyed during World War Two and the modern buildings that have replaced them say nothing for the ability of those responsible for their design. The Dolphin Hotel, however, where Jane Austen danced, remains in all its Georgian glory.

Looking north along the High Street from the entrance of the Dolphin Hotel after the 1941 Blitz, showing that all the west side of the High Street, from its junction with West Street, had been destroyed. The only remaining building is the Leeds Permanent Building Society, near the junction with Castle Lane.

The Duke of Wellington public house in Bugle Street, *c.*1941, built during the 15th century and known as the Brewhouse in 1490. It became the Shipwright's Arms in 1771 but took its present name in 1815, after the Battle of Waterloo. It lost its top floor during the Blitz but was rebuilt to its original proportions in 1961.

An early 1950s view of the Leeds Permanent Building Society and S.W. Silver, armed services outfitters, at 164 High Street, next to the tiny Castle Lane. The Midland Bank is on the other corner of the lane and the Gaiety Cinema can just be seen, with the equally small Albion Place sandwiched between the two.

The Leeds Permanent Building Society building fell victim to post-war redevelopment and has been replaced by a betting shop, with adjacent new premises built on the former bombed site. The Midland is now the HSBC bank and the Gaiety Cinema, closed in 1956, has been replaced by nondescript offices.

Part of the post-war High Street reconstruction, this large and impressive furniture store, shown in 1961, covered every aspect of house furnishing and had a good reputation. They stocked products of good quality and catered for the upper end of the market, but eventually found it uneconomical to remain here.

Half of the former furniture store became the main High Street Post Office and the other followed what seems to be an unstoppable trend of converting large main street premises into massive public houses-cum-restaurants. Brannigans had the additional attraction of 'cavorting', but this did not prevent it closing!

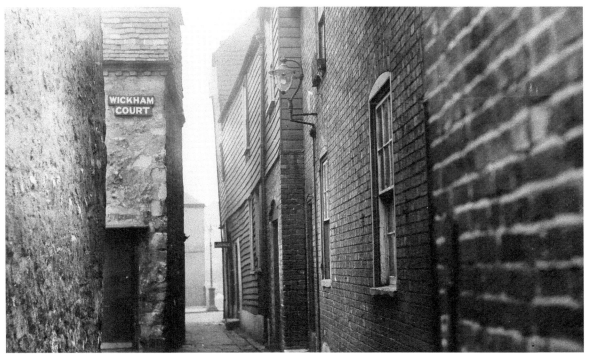

Wickham Court, leading off Vyse Lane, was in one of the town's poorest districts and was not included in the main water and sewerage system, giving rise to the ever-present threat of cholera. Vyse Lane is of mediaeval origin and was called Beneytes Lane in the 13th century and Fortis Lane in the 14th century.

The 1893 Dilapidated Buildings Report marked Wickham Court for demolition, but in fact it survived until the slum clearance programme of the 1930s and post-war flats now occupy the site. The Duke of Wellington public house is on the right, and the view has opened up Bugle Street to show the Westgate.

The Pineapple Inn at No. 11, St Michael's Square, is shown in this 1896 watercolour by W. Cooper. It is the subject of an unsubstantiated story that John Sturdy, one of its landlords and a staunch Roman Catholic, held church services here before St Joseph's Catholic Church was built on the other side of the square.

The public house and adjoining premises, as far as Simnel Street, were all demolished in the slum clearance programme of 1898, and the very large St Michael's Municipal Common Lodging House was built on the site. This was, in turn, demolished in 1972 and replaced by pleasant council properties in 1983.

Simnel Street by W. Cooper, *c.*1896, looking down towards the sea. Simnel cakes, probably from the Latin 'simila', meaning fine wheaten flour, had been known from mediaeval times, and this area was thought to be the bakers' quarters. The small lane on the right led to Lansdowne Place and then through to Castle Square.

The old properties have been replaced by attractive modern buildings, in a style that is in keeping with the mediaeval history of the area. The shoreline was reclaimed in the 1930s for the New Docks extension and there is no longer access to the sea. The Quays 'Eddie Read' Swimming Baths now takes up the former view.

The Old Candleworks in Simnel Street at the junction with West Street, *c.*1896, by W. Cooper. This building was originally a mediaeval house and then a public house before becoming a candleworks. It then became a home once again and at the time of this painting was occupied by three families.

Much has changed over the past 100 years. The old buildings were demolished soon after the Cooper watercolour was made, and World War Two bombing and the construction of the Portland Terrace/Castle Way ring road truncated the junction with West Street. The smart houses have been built only recently.

This etching of West Street and St Michael's Church was made by the local artist, etcher and sculptor Frank McFadden, who was active between 1880 and 1900. The late 11th-century church was restored in 1872 and the spire heightened in 1880. The properties were swept away by bombing and post-war development.

Blue Anchor Lane, just before the slum clearance programme of the 1890s. It ran alongside Tudor House, now a museum, from St Michael's Square to the Western Shore. The houses, together with the buildings to their north, were replaced by St Michael's Lodging House in 1899. This was demolished in 1972.

Swimming baths were first built on Western Esplanade in 1891, but by the 1960s they were 'no longer fit for purpose'. This photograph shows the New Baths under construction lower down Western Esplanade in 1961. However, by the 1980s it was said to be costly to run because it was heated with oil-fired boilers.

The New Baths closed in 1992 as the facilities were said to be inadequate. This Quays 'Eddie Read' swimming and diving complex was opened on the same site in June 1999 and cost almost £10 million. With paired spring boards and five diving platforms it is said to be the finest in the south of England.

Southampton.

This northern section of Western Esplanade, between Manchester Street and Fitzhugh Street, was called Weymouth Terrace and is shown *c.*1870, before the 1891 Corporation Baths or 1903 power station were built. It faced the open water of the River Test and gave a clear view of Marchwood on the opposite bank.

Western Esplanade is now free from housing and the Corporation Baths and power station have also disappeared. An Asda superstore and a large block of student accommodation have been built on the site of Weymouth Terrace, and an overhead walkway gives access to a multi-storey car park on the Baths site.

This National Provincial Bank was built in 1932 at 194 Above Bar Street by Portsmouth builders A.E. Porter. The steelwork was by local firm Pollock & Brown, who proudly boasted that only British steel was used. The building is now Southampton's newest contemporary dance club, the White House.

This public house, originally called the Plumber's Arms, at 22 Bargate Street, on the corner of Western Esplanade, dates back to the early 1850s. It became the Old Tower Inn in the 1870s and the Old Arundel Tower Hotel in 1899. When it was demolished in the late 1960s the ancient Arundel Tower was fully revealed.

This 1990s view of the lower end of Portland Terrace, looking towards the Civic Centre, shows the full extent of the impressive Arundel Towers office blocks, constructed in 1968. On the right is the *Daily Echo* office block, built on the site of the old Coliseum building. Work is starting on a new pedestrian bridge.

The twin tower blocks were removed in 1997 to develop the West Quay Shopping Centre and the covered entrance from the High Street Precinct, bridging a lowered and redesigned Portland Terrace. The pedestrian bridge, leading to the ancient Arundel Tower, is complete and the *Daily Echo* has relocated to Redbridge.

Lower Above Bar in 1947, showing the dramatic effect of the Luftwaffe's *blitzkrieg*. The heart was taken out of the town and the residents were struggling to come to terms with post-war austerity. A small temporary branch of the Halifax Building Society, on the corner of Hanover Buildings, is the first sign of recovery.

By 1953 redevelopment is getting under way and more stores, albeit small and temporary, are beginning to make an appearance. Building materials are still scarce, but the pace is picking up. Traffic is also increasing, and the Corporation tramcars have been replaced by buses.

It is now 1957 and reconstruction work is virtually complete. The busy Above Bar is a fine shopping centre, with wide pavements and ample parking on both sides of the road. The lower west side, however, still consists of single-storey temporary shops. The Civic Centre clock tower is visible in the upper left.

This 2007 view from the top of the Bargate shows a different picture. The area is now fully pedestrianised and the Civic Centre clock tower is partially obscured by taller modern stores. The Halifax Building Society at the top of Hanover Buildings was a McDonald's outlet for many years, but is now unoccupied.

The north side of Hanover Buildings, from the High Street, *c.*1920. Left to right are: Jacob Cohen & Sons, tailors, naval and military outfitters; Rose Needlework Agency (Arts and Crafts, Agents for Sandow Corsets); Mrs M. Crouch, furniture dealer; Tea Rooms; and the scaffolding around new offices for Wm Burrough Hill.

The north side in 1924. Left to right are: Barclays Bank; the Hanover Arms; Gem Tailors; Rose Agency; J.H. Whiteside, pianoforte and gramophones; John Rose, insurance broker; and Henty & Hill Treasure House, fine arts and curios. William Burrough Hill, auctioneer and estate agent, has completed his new offices.

Henry Wright, from Norfolk, started trading as a glass merchant at 3 Hanover Buildings in 1862 and moved over to these premises on the south side the following year. The business was taken over by his son Edward in 1914, followed by Reginald in 1944, Michael in 1962 and Paul and Kim in 1987.

The entire north side of Hanover Buildings (right) was destroyed by bombing in World War Two and was also later cordoned off for a while when an unexploded bomb was discovered. William Burrough Hill died in 1941 and E.R. Wright and Son (these initials have been retained) moved to Millbrook Road in 1987.

The upper end of the High Street, c.1895, showing the south face of the Norman Bargate that guarded the entrance to the old town. The Roman-style statue in the niche is, in fact, of George III and was placed there in 1809. The vehicles seen through the arch are horsedrawn, as electric trams did not arrive until 1900.

The eastern side of the Bargate was opened up in 1932 to avoid the congestion of two-way traffic through the restricted central archway. The Bargate Circus was completed in 1938, to allow traffic on both sides, but the entire area is now fully pedestrianised, allowing these regular, popular markets to take place.

The lower end of Above Bar in 1931, at the junction with Hanover Buildings, showing that W. Parkhouse, watchmaker and jeweller, has a 4s in the £1 discount sale (20%) and Curry's Cycle Co. is selling all goods at half price. The premises are to be demolished because of the imminent Bargate Improvement Scheme.

The scheme allowed traffic to circle this eastern side of the ancient Bargate, which was blocking access to the High Street, and this was later extended to completely encircle the structure. W. Parkhouse moved to 96 Above Bar and later became Parkhouse & Wyatt.

Above Bar Street, *c.*1910, looking north, with the Royal Hotel on the right. The hotel dates back to the 1820s but its licence lapsed in 1919. Next door are the *Southampton Times* offices, on the corner of Pound Tree Road. On the left, at No. 61, near Portland Street, is the White Hart Inn, which dates back to 1783.

The Royal Hotel building was later shared by Woolworth's Store and the Gas Company, but was destroyed in the war. The White Hart Inn was renamed Scullards in the 1930s, one of three premises so called over the years, but it was also destroyed in the Blitz. Woolworths, shown here, has now closed and left the precinct.

Looking west along Pound Tree Road in March 1960, with Jackson the tailor occupying the corner of Above Bar. The Odeon is showing *Journey to the Centre of the Earth*. Further down Pound Tree Road is Allans, confectioner and tobacconist, and J.T.M. Cox's, hairdressing salon.

The former tailor's shop on the corner has undergone many changes of use and is now the city's main Nationwide Building Society premises. The small shops and private accommodation have been replaced by large betting shops, and this lower section of Above Bar is partially pedestrianised.

The Odeon cinema opened in June 1934 and was known as the Regal until April 1945. It is shown here in May 1962, when it reopened after the installation of a wide screen and stereophonic sound. Next door is the traditional and pleasant looking Above Bar Church of Christ (Evangelical Free Church), erected in 1883.

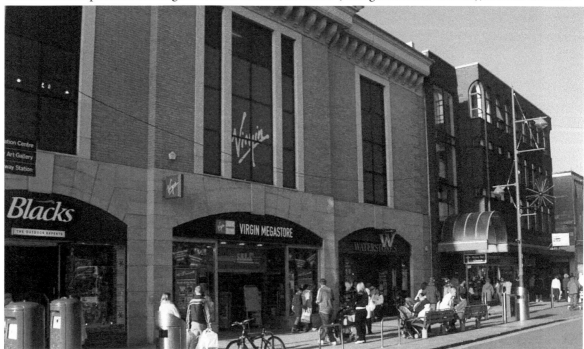

The Odeon cinema closed for good in September 1993 and was replaced by Blacks Leisure, a Virgin Megastore and a Waterstones book store the following year. Now known simply as the Above Bar Church, the traditional church building was demolished and rebuilt in 1979, with shops taking up the ground floor.

Southampton's Woolston Vickers-Supermarine works was a principal factory for producing the famous Spitfire, but it was completely destroyed by the Luftwaffe in September 1940. This meant the dispersal of production, and the author recalls seeing Spitfire parts being manufactured in this Vincents Walk garage.

The Percy Hendy garage and showrooms served as the main Ford dealer for vehicles and accessories. Although they later left these premises, the Hendy Group remains a dominant car dealer in the area. The building is now a supermarket for bargain goods of all kinds, with club premises on the lower floor.

An immediate post-war view of the effects of bomb damage in Above Bar Street. In spite of the severe damage to the upper floors, both Halfords cycle shop and the Freeman Hardy Willis shoe shop are still in business. The Sussex Hotel at 86–88 was well known in the town and dated from the mid-19th century.

The business premises now have a variety of new owners, and the popular Sussex Hotel, which was on the corner of the narrow Sussex Terrace, surrendered its licence in February 1967 and was demolished soon after. This section of Above Bar Street has now been partially pedestrianised.

The east side of Above Bar Street in 1920, just north of Pound Tree Road (right). From left to right are: Bishop Brothers' shoe shop (82); Arthur Martell, watchmaker (80); Fred Bailey, florist and greengrocer (78); C.W. Batten, tailors (76); and, on the corner of Pound Tree Road, Burt Weston, costumier (72–74).

The shops have changed considerably. From left to right now are: Priceless, shoe shop; Select, fashions; Dolland & Aitchison, opticians; Pearl Harbour, Chinese restaurant; Chelsea Building Society; Gamestation; Pickett & Pursers, jewellers; and the Nationwide Building Society on the corner of Pound Tree Road.

Above Bar in 1954, showing, from left to right: the Church of Christ on the corner of Ogle Road; the Royal Southampton Yacht Club (on the corner of Manchester Street; various shops in the Prudential Buildings block, including G.A. Dunn, hatters; Van Allan costumiers; Phillips shoe shop; and Meakers outfitters.

The Above Bar Church of Christ has been rebuilt over a block of shops, the striking Royal Southampton Yacht Club has been demolished and Manchester Street is now the east entrance of the Marlands Shopping Centre. The gap in the Prudential Buildings has also been filled to form one block of smaller shops.

Taken from the Civic Centre in the 1960s, this shows the Rose Gardens and illuminated fountain that formed a roundabout in front of the much-valued bus station. To the right is the Lord Louis public house, opened by Louis Mountbatten in 1960 and built on the site of the bombed Brewery Bar premises.

The Marlands office block on the left, built on the site of the Grand Theatre in 1962, was complemented by the Marlands Shopping Centre in 1989. This not only occupied the site of the former bus station, but also the Lord Louis public house, which closed in 1987. Windsor Terrace was also lost in the development.

The Forum Cinema in Above Bar opened in June 1935 and could seat 1,798 patrons. Reginald Porter Brown was famous locally as the cinema's organist, playing its Compton organ. Its name was changed to the ABC in 1959 and to the Cannon in 1986. This photograph was taken in 1954, and it closed in February 1991.

The cinema was slightly damaged in a raid in November 1940, when an unexploded bomb dropped into it. The author was given a piece of the fuse mechanism from the bomb by his father, who was a Police Officer on duty at the time. Restaurants have now replaced not only the cinema but also the adjoining shops.

129 Above Bar Street, at the junction with Gibbs Road, in 1941. In the 19th century this was part of the imposing Anglesea Terrace, named after the Marquis of Anglesea (1768–1854). No. 129, occupied by Lewis Price Hosiers and Young's Hairdressers, was the only part to survive 1930s modernisation and the Blitz.

In 1492 Henry VII granted £50 towards the making of a new wall on the west side of the town. Several private persons also contributed at this time, among them Lord Arundel, whose name was given to this tower at the north-west corner. When this scene was painted, in 1896, the tower was used as a home.

120 Above Bar Street, on the corner of New Road and backing onto Andrew's Park, was originally Moira House, named after the Earl of Moira, who embarked from Southampton in 1794 during the war with France. It was once the offices of the Co-operative Permanent Building Society, later the Nationwide.

The Information Kiosk in Watts Park was a very popular feature, but the public shelter became the haunt of the less fortunate members of society and was removed. The Information Bureau was relocated to Civic Centre Road, and the site is now an entrance and path to the park.

A pre-1900 view of Prospect Place, at the junction of upper Above Bar with Commercial Road. The date is determined by the horse-drawn tram travelling towards London Road, as the town's first electric tram did not run until 1900. The castellated tower was 'Ellyetts Folly', the home of a Portsmouth businessman.

The electric tramcars have come and gone and, although many of the buildings have changed, the pair of bay windows next to the former 'Ellyetts Folly' (now a 'Beatnic Emporium') can still be seen. Further down, the popular large Tyrrell & Green store lies empty, the firm having moved to the West Quay Centre.

This 1872 photograph of Cumberland Place, between The Polygon and Grosvenor Square, taken from Watts Park, shows the genteel nature of the area and the fine houses. One later became St Hilda's High School, run by Miss G.F. Henry, and another was the home of the vicar of St Peter's Church, in Commercial Road.

Because of the dense foliage in Watts Park, it is not possible to take a photograph from the same position. The 72-room Southampton Park Hotel now occupies the site of St Hilda's High School, but in spite of the large modern office blocks some of the buildings beyond the hotel remain basically unchanged.

This western end of Cumberland Place, leading up to the Royal Hotel at the far right of the picture, was home to chartered surveyors, insurance companies and estate agents, as well as a large number of physicians and surgeons. This mid-1960s photograph was taken when the bomb-damaged Nos 2–4 were up for sale.

Nos 1–4 Cumberland Place were replaced by the 12-storey office complex 'Queens Keep', now leased to various organisations but originally constructed for HM Revenue & Customs as their main Southampton headquarters. The Royal Hotel is now the Southampton Park Hotel, here partially obscured by trees.

Looking up Bedford Place, from near the junction with Cumberland Place, one can see the Pilgrim Coaches offices and coach station that provided extremely useful travel to all parts of the country. The services of the Grosvenor Square Royal Blue coach station, via the access road in front of the offices, were also available.

Both coach stations were demolished and not reinstated, but replaced by large office blocks. Sadly, a much smaller scale replacement coach station, located in Western Esplanade, has no garage facilities. Bedford Place remains an interesting shopping area, with some character, and a lively student population.

Waterloo Terrace in 1963, from Bedford Place to London Road, with the well known Moonrakers restaurant at No. 2, next to the alleyway called Waterloo Chambers. On the corner, barely visible, is the Walpamur Company, paint manufacturers. The terrace dates back to the late 1830s.

The side of the Red Lion public house, on the left, is unchanged, but there has been a dramatic transformation of the entire area. The 1830s properties and Waterloo Chambers have all been demolished to fully expose Salisbury Street, where an office block has been erected on the corner with Waterloo Terrace.

Amoy Street in 1970, looking towards Bedford Place. In 1964 Mr and Mrs Bryan Baker purchased No. 29 (the house with the low white wall and scooters parked outside) for £1,250. It had three bedrooms, a sitting room, an outside toilet in a small back yard and a large copper sink. The terrace was built in the early 1840s.

The entire terrace was demolished shortly after the earlier view was taken, and this council car park was built on the site. No. 29, at 2007 prices, would now fetch between £150,000 and £165,000! The NHS Bedford House Day Centre is at the lower end of the street, just below where this photograph was taken.

Carlton Road, looking towards Bedford Place and the junction with Carlton Crescent, in 1951. The 33-bedroomed Carlton Hotel can be seen on the left of the picture, and on the opposite corner, at 56 Bedford Place, is the well-known piano supplier H.J. Klitz & Son, and Mr Anthony Zorab's dental surgery.

St Anne's Secondary School, previously known as St Anne's Roman Catholic Convent School, with over 1,100 girl pupils and adjacent to the former Carlton Hotel, has now built a large annexe on the hotel site. 56 Bedford Place is now occupied by private apartments and the Wilton Lodge medical and dental practice.

A view calculated to arouse nostalgia for all Southampton football fans – the Archers Road entrance of the Dell, the club's home since 3 September 1898 when they played Brighton United. The club's peak came in 1976 when the team won the FA Cup, an event celebrated by the entire city.

Southampton Football Club moved into its new stadium, the £32 million state-of-the-art Friends Provident St Mary's Stadium in Britannia Road, for the start of the 2001–02 English Premiership soccer season in August 2001. Their move meant that this massive Barratt Homes complex was built on the old site.

The junction of Shirley Road, Commercial Road, Nelson Hill and Millbrook Road, known as Four Posts Hill, in 1960. A group of shops can be seen in lower Shirley Road. They include: Charles Du-Gay, antique dealer; Beeching, commercial printer; Thomas Ingleton, perambulator dealer; and Wilkes & Co., drapers.

The Anglo-City House block of offices has now been built on the site of the former group of shops. Two roundabouts have also taken the place of the traffic lights. In ancient times this was where the main west road from Southampton met at the point where the Romsey and Redbridge roads parted.

The Shirley Road end of Millbrook Road in 1910, with the Four Posts Mission to the right of the picture. The 1899 Directory shows the Mission at No. 33, also occupied by William Herepath, bootmaker; Miss Newman at No. 35; and, at the extreme left, the house of William Fran Bruce, physician and surgeon.

The A33 by-pass has now taken the place of Millbrook Road as the main west road from Southampton, and the old cottages on the north side of the road have been replaced by pleasant modern housing. Bourne Road, called Osbourne Road when the earlier photograph was taken, is to the left of the picture, just out of sight.

Freemantle Congregational Church at the junction of Shirley Road and Roberts Road. This church complex was built in 1884–85 when the Congregationalists, Southampton's oldest Nonconformist body, first extended into the suburbs to serve an ever-expanding local population.

The church was destroyed by bombing in World War Two and a new church, now the Freemantle United Reformed Church, built further up the road in the 1950s. Southampton's Congregationalists were founded by the Revd Robinson, former rector of All Saints, who was ejected for Nonconformity in 1662.

The Victoria Inn, Beatrice Road, at the junction with Randolph Street, in 1968. It was known as the Brewer's Arms until 1899, when the road was Victoria Road. This became Beatrice Road in 1924, following the absorption of Woolston into Southampton in 1920, when the Woolston Victoria Road retained its name.

The Victoria Inn closed in August 1972 and was later demolished, with this attractive modern terrace later built on the site. The plaque on the wall states that the row is called 'Strawberry Fields' to commemorate the market gardening history of Shirley, which did not become part of Southampton until 1895.

The west side of upper Shirley Road, at the junction with Villiers Road, *c.*1960, with the popular Downeys drapery store on the corner. Next door is the Two Eyes restaurant, then Holdens, with what appear to be large dolls' houses on the forecourt, and another Downeys shop. Further down is South Hants Motors.

There has been no dramatic change to the buildings, but a complete change of the occupying businesses. There is no longer a Downeys in the city. The corner shop is now 'Cash Converters' and the smaller shop is the Bright Water Inn. In between are the Kachina Chinese restaurant and R.C. Payne, undertakers.

Numbers 11–3 Cannon Street, near its junction with Shirley High Street, to the right. Built around 1860, this used to be called Pound Street, where the Shirley Pound was located. It lost out to Bitterne's Pound Street in the name changes of 1924, after eastern areas were absorbed into Southampton in 1920.

The original Cannon Street was very long, running from Shirley High Street to St James' Road, but it is now only a short section as far as Vincent Street and devoid of houses. Small business premises have replaced the terraced homes, demolished in the 1960s, and there is no longer access from Shirley High Street.

Numbers 32 and 34 Cannon Street, Shirley, at the junction with Vincent Street, in 1961. On the corner is the Good Intent off-licence, formerly the Red Lion public house, which closed in the 1930s. It was then a radio shop for many years before reverting to an off-licence.

Extensive redevelopment in the 1960s resulted in a small car park replacing the Cannon Street buildings and small business premises extending down Cannon Street towards Shirley High Street. The tree, which did not exist in 1961, has grown considerably over the past 45 years!

Nos 38–46 Howard's Grove, at the junction with Vincent Street, in 1961. It is shown on the 1840 Tithe Map but with no houses and unnamed. The earliest buildings, on the west side of the street, are pre-1865, but this terrace, north of Vincent Street, is on the site of the old Shirley Gasworks and was built after 1883.

The Shirley Gasworks opened in 1859 but closed in 1869 and the land was sold for development in 1883. The Victorian street was demolished in the mid-1960s as part of the Shirley Clearance Area, and the entire district is now covered with modern houses and a large multi-storey block of apartments.

The children are posing for their photograph across the mouth of Church Street, Shirley, in 1907, with no thought of possible danger from traffic. The tall pipe on the left is a 'stink pipe', which carried noxious fumes from the drain system. St James's Church, dating from 1836, can just be seen in the background.

Shirley Baptist Church can now be seen on the left and, although the lower shops on the right are basically the same, the upper stretch of the street was extensively redeveloped under the Shirley No. 1 Clearance Area Scheme of 1961. Considerable traffic is now liable to enter from Shirley High Street.

Nos 31 and 29 Church Street in 1961, at the junction with Vincent Street. No. 31 was occupied by the Noyce Brothers, haulage contractors, and the adjacent 29 by Francis Doling's popular lending library. Mr Doling also diversified into various leather and travel goods to augment his income.

The building changes have not been too dramatic, but they nevertheless show the change in social outlook over the past half century. Small corner shops supplying a variety of services are now a rarity and businesses have to be far more security conscious.

The Star Inn, 87 Church Street, Shirley, in 1961, on the corner of Cambridge Street and adjacent to Nos 85 to 77. Originally only a beer house, it dates back to the 1860s and did not obtain a full licence until 1960. Scrase's Star Brewery held the original lease, but this later passed to Strong's Romsey Brewery.

The Star Inn closed in 1965 and was demolished soon after. These flats were built on the site and along Church Street. Cambridge Street disappeared during the development. Nearby, to the left just out of sight, are the Barlow & Ellyett homes, originally a poor asylum founded by the Rev. Herbert Smith in 1841.

The Lion Inn at 14 Wellington Street, on the junction with Stratton Road, in 1962, after a snow fall. It was originally known as the Old Lion Inn when it held a beer licence before 1869, but it became the Lion Inn in February 1908. Owned by Mew Langton's Newport Brewery, it was not granted a full licence until 1954.

The Lion Inn was demolished in January 1968, during the development of the Shirley Clearance Area scheme, and Wellington Street entirely disappeared during the process. The site is now occupied by the grounds of the Stratton Road Wordsworth Infant School, which has around 180 pupils.

OLD SHIRLEY · VILLAGE. 11

A pre-war view of the 'Old Shirley' junction from Maybush Hill, looking up Romsey Road towards Shirley. The Old Thatched House Inn is on the left and the chimney belching smoke is that of the Heathfield Brewery in Winchester Road. Redbridge Hill is on the right, and was the route to the west from Shirley.

The Old Thatched House Inn, Southampton's only thatched public house, was a beer house in the 1890s. The dual carriageway Tebourba Way, opened in 1953 and named after the Hampshire Regiment's North African 1942 battle honour, is now just beyond Redbridge Hill and has replaced it as the route to the west.

The Medina Motor Works, 59 Winchester Road, on the corner of Medina Road, in 1958, owned by Mr G.R. Blake. Safety considerations would now prohibit petrol pumps so close to the road. Police pillar No. 10 gave direct contact with Shirley Police Station and was regularly used by the author as a young PC.

The corner garage and service station is now called 'Central Tyre' and the outside petrol pumps no longer exist, allowing the street lamp to be realigned. The police pillars, which were also a direct contact line for the general public, were removed when radio handsets became available in the 1960s.

Mr Sid Sales proudly stands outside his thriving business at the junction of Shayer Road and Moreland Road in Shirley in 1929. He is promoting fine Dutch cheese at 9d a pound as well as Oxo, Rinso and HP sauce. Hampshire Cricket Club is also advertised as playing Yorkshire at the County Ground in Northlands Road.

The grocery side of the business gradually fell away as the licensed premises part became more important. It became the Prince of Wales Feathers off-licence, but this also fell victim to the growth of the supermarkets. Shayer Road was truncated when part was taken over by Bellemoor School for playing fields.

The Bassett Hotel, 111 Burgess Road, in January 2005. Built in 1871 on the corner of Burgess Road and Butterfield Road, its first landlord had the grand name of George Washington Jones. It once had a bear pit, complete with real bears, and was the original home of the Concorde Club, famous for its jazz concerts.

The hotel was completely refurbished and partially rebuilt in 1972 at a cost of £80,000 to become a Berni Steak House. Within a few months of the 2005 photograph being taken the Bassett Hotel closed for good and was demolished. The Sunrise Senior Living complex, above, was then built on the site.

Nos 468–480 on the east side of Portswood Road, near the junction with Belgrave Road. They were also known as Nos 1–6 Brook Terrace and the corner shop, No. 468, was a newsagent, confectioner and tobacconists, owned by a Miss Alma Bailey. Further down are a butchers, wine merchant and bakers.

Brook Terrace was demolished and replaced by the Belgravia Car Sales forecourt, using the former address of 468 Portswood Road. The shops further down remain, but have all changed ownership and use since the 1967 photograph was taken.

Swaythling Farm, at the junction of High Road and Wide Lane, in 1941, also known as Brown's Farm after Mr H. Brown, who occupied the farm in the 19th century. In the left background is a partial view of The Grange, a 16th-century Grade II listed building, where Oliver Cromwell once visited his son Richard.

This view is again taken from Wide Lane and shows the site of The Grange on the left. It was purchased by the Southampton Corporation in 1965 and demolished in 1974. On the right is Grange Court, a block of flats on the site of Brown's Farm, which was demolished following a fire in the 1960s.

Brown's Farm being demolished, with the view this time from High Road looking towards the junction of Wide Lane and Mansbridge Road, known as Westfield Corner. The remaining tall chimneys are very similar to those on The Grange before it was demolished. Note the small police contact pillar at the road junction.

Grange Court, seen on the left, was built in the 1980s by Swaythling Housing Society. It is designed for elderly tenants who can live independently but who benefit from the provided support and services. It also offers leasehold owner-occupied accommodation for those over 55. Wessex Lane is on the right.

This building, which became Portswood Police Station, was originally built in Portswood Road in 1849 as Starling Villas. Purchased by the Southampton Watch Committee in 1873, it was altered to provide cells and office accommodation. Next door is a shed that was part of the original Victorian Corporation tram depot.

Although plans for the station's replacement were made as far back as 1938, they were deferred due to the war, and the modern Portswood Police Station was built on a new site in St Denys Road in 1965. The tram depot shed has been replaced by a realigned St Denys Road and the station by the bus depot grounds.

A 1966 view of 147 to 155 Bevois Valley Road, just south of the junction with Forster Road. The Unit Books shop was formerly the premises of Sydney Charles Brewer, boot repairer, adjoining the showroom of Charles Lanham, furniture dealer and remover. Boots the Chemists was on the corner with Forster Road.

The shop premises and houses were demolished in the 1960s as part of a road widening and clearance programme. To the right of the photograph, just out of sight, is Thomas Lewis Way. It was named after a late popular local Labour Alderman and reduces the heavy traffic that would otherwise pass through Portswood.

Looking up Bevois Valley Road towards Portswood in 1910, with the Mount Hotel at No. 67 on the left, on the corner with Ancasta Road. The public house dates back to the 1850s, when George Hellier was the licensee. The 1878 Drink Map shows a beer house on this site, then called Alliance Place.

The Mount Hotel, a Watney's house, closed in 1958 when its licence was transferred to the newly constructed Park Tavern in Pound Tree Road. It was used as a scrap metal dealer's office for some time, but it was later demolished and modern flats built on the site. The electric tram service ceased in 1949.

The service station of A.E. Hayter & Son in Bevois Valley Road, at the junction with Earls Road, in 1958. This was one of many small petrol stations in the city where, at that time, an attendant had to fill the car personally. In the right background, past the junction with Kingsbury Road, is A.E. Holt, ironmongers.

The small petrol station was one of many that succumbed to the competition from cheaper petrol available from larger outlets. It is now an empty plot, next to Heli-Beds at 47–65 Bevois Valley Road, who boast they can deliver a bed the same day it is ordered. A.E. Holt's premises were destroyed by fire in the 1960s.

The junction of Lodge Road and Bevois Hill, Portswood. A small tobacconists and confectioners shop at No. 8 Lodge Road was on the right, behind the advertising hoardings. These were on a former bomb site. The shop was once managed by the author's parents. Directly opposite was a small Esso filling station.

The road junction has been reconstructed to cater for the increased traffic serving the nearby modern Thomas Lewis Way dual carriageway, and the advertising site has been extensively redeveloped, as has the former confectionery shop. The Esso garage has become one of the Tesco Express stores.

Nos 89–93 Mount Pleasant Road, near the junction with Bevois Valley Road, on the left. George Thresher, a 25-year-old fireman on the *Titanic* in 1912, lived opposite at 28 Mount Pleasant Road, further down towards Derby Road. He was one of the fortunate ones who was saved (in lifeboat No. 14).

The houses have been swept away and replaced by the car park of Heritage Windows, a glass-cutting company, and Hodges Autolec, dealing in car security and towbars. The building on the corner, at 30 Bevois Valley Road, is the Dungeon nightclub.

A 1967 view of the Number One Inn, 76 Mount Pleasant Road, so named because in the early 20th century its address was No. 1 Spring Place. It only had a beer licence in 1869 but received a full licence in 1961. This was suspended in March 1969 and the inn was gutted by fire, possibly in an arson attack, in May that year.

The Number One Inn was demolished after the disastrous fire and the site cleared. It was later made into the Mount Pleasant Play Area for local children and the vehicle park for the adjoining J.S. Cars, a vehicle body repair workshop. Nearby is the Mount Pleasant Junior School, attended by the author in 1938.

Nos 260–256 Derby Road, after a parachute mine attack on 10 April 1941. This damage is remembered by the author, who lived in the adjacent Northumberland Road at the time of the attack. The houses were built in the late 19th century on the east side of the road, not far from Mount Pleasant School.

The swishing of the parachute mine was heard by the author, who was blown out of his bed by the explosion and his home also rendered uninhabitable. The damaged houses were later demolished, and the site is now the enclosed playground of the adjacent Maytree Nursery and Junior School.

The foundation stone of the Royal South Hants Hospital, formerly the Royal South Hampshire Infirmary, was laid on 10 July 1843 and its chapel, on the left, was built in 1857 on the corner of Fanshawe Street and Exmoor Road. Fanshawe Street is now only a small cul-de-sac and Exmoor Road no longer exists.

The chapel, now inside the hospital grounds as the two roads have vanished, closed in 1998, and the adjoining wing of the old RSH was demolished to provide car parking space. The hospital is now also a Community Health Campus, with access to a wide range of primary care-led services.

Upper St Mary's Road, near the junction with Onslow Road, with part of the Newtown Inn on the left. After refurbishment in 1984 it reopened as the Bitter End and in 1993 changed to the Oliver Goldsmith. Next door is a restaurant, then a tobacconist, radio/TV shop, and other shops, just before Brinton's Terrace.

The Newtown Inn is now called H_2O, and is painted a vivid blue. As part of the changing social scene next door is a Pizza Parlour, then a Polish and Eastern European food store and a mobile phone shop, with the rest boarded up. A new road has also been created at this point to join Onslow Road with the Inner Avenue.

Looking down on Upper St Mary's Road, the Territorial Army Drill Hall is on the left, on the corner of Clovelly Road. Built in 1889, it was the headquarters of the 1st Hants Volunteer Artillery. In the centre is the Co-operative Society drapery, outfitting, furnishing, funeral, boots and restaurant building, built in 1934.

This photograph was taken from the Orion's Point Student and Keyworkers block that has been built in front of the former large Gas Board office block. The Co-operative building has now been demolished and the area is awaiting further development. The buildings in lower Compton Walk can now be seen.

The west side of St Mary's Road, between Northam Street on the left and Bellevue Street on the right. Hillier's furniture shop on the corner, at No. 65, was shown as Sidney House on the 1845–46 town map. No. 65a is occupied by St Mary's Glass, next door to the former Antelope Hotel at No. 66.

The previous 1961 view has changed somewhat. It is now part of the Charlotte Place gyratory system, with all the properties long vanished. The rear office block was originally constructed for the Southern Gas Company, but it is now shared by many organisations. In front is the Orion Point accommodation block.

Northam Street, looking west from St Mary's Road to East Park Terrace, and showing, from left to right, Nos 2–11 on the north side of the road. It was probably built in the early 1820s, and in 1850 Phillip Brannon called it 'an assemblage of Humble dwellings at the back of Compton Walk'.

The earlier photograph was taken in 1963 and the properties were demolished soon afterwards to create the Charlotte Place car park. Nothing now remains of the road, other than this front entrance from St Mary's Road. The former car park is now underneath the Jurys Inn, seen in the background.

The east side of Dorset Street in 1961, between Bellevue Street on the far left and Northam Street on the right. The buildings are, from right to left: Park House (the white building on the corner of Northam Street); East Park Cottage; Nos 1 and 2 St Andrew's Cottages; and Dundee Cottage (on the corner of Bellevue Street).

Dorset Street is now a dual carriageway, the A33 leading north to join the Avenue and the M3 motorway. Both Bellevue Street and Northam Street have vanished beneath the Charlotte Place gyratory road system, large multi-storey office blocks and the north side of the Jurys Inn.

Continuing on from the previous set of photographs, Dorset Street becomes East Park Terrace from its junction with Northam Street. This row was originally called Brunswick Terrace and was built *c.*1840. The Marston's East Park Inn at No. 39 had been a beer house since the 1860s and was formerly a lodging house.

The former Brunswick Terrace, Nos 35–42 East Park Terrace, has been completely replaced by the massive Jurys Inn, plumb in the centre of the Charlotte Place gyratory system. The former properties led right up to Compton Walk on their right, the upper stretch of which is now also long vanished.

Following on from the previous East Park Terrace photograph, this view continues to the junction with Compton Walk and shows, from left to right, Nos 37–34 East Park Terrace. When this photograph was taken in 1961 the offices on the corner were occupied by estate agents Medway & Fraser.

In common with the other photographs taken in this vicinity, the properties were all demolished in the early 1960s to create the Charlotte Place car park and new gyratory road system. Charlotte Place was, in turn, transformed by the 2005 construction of the 270-bedroom Jurys Inn in its centre island car park.

Nos 8–11 on the north side of Compton Walk, built in the 1830s and leading down to St Mary's Road to the right. This section was known as Charlotte Place and has given its name to the modern developments in the area. These photographs were taken in 1961, just prior to the redevelopment.

The opposite side of Compton Walk to the preceding view, but still looking down to St Mary's Road on the left. Nos 34–38 are shown, as is the store of William Dibben, the well-known local builders' merchants. His son, Alderman Frank Dibben, who was Mayor in 1948, later controlled the business.

The author was delighted to find this 1961 photograph of Nos 30–35 Compton Walk in the archives as he lived in No. 34, the first protruding house on the right, from 1941 to 1943. The family was evacuated there from their home in nearby Northumberland Road after it was almost destroyed by a parachute mine.

This is all that is left of Compton Walk: just the public house seen on the left, on the corner of St Mary's Road. The underground Charlotte Place car park is now underneath the massive Jurys Inn. On the left is the private car park of the Southampton Medina Mosque and Al-Nisaa Association.

This 1961 photograph shows the junction of the top of Compton Walk with St Andrew's Road. The author well remembers purchasing his weekly ration of sweets from Mr West's corner shop in 1942, when he was 10 years old. A large bomb dropped at the rear, in St Andrew's Road, the following year.

There is no remaining trace of this part of Compton Walk and the top of St Andrew's Road, which vanished under the Charlotte Place development and gyratory system. The modern housing on the right, at the top of the now diverted St Andrew's Road, is close to the former location of Mr West's sweet shop.

The Bird Aviary *c*.1955, in the north-west corner of Andrew's Park, close to the Rock Gardens. It was a popular attraction from about 1904 and housed a wide variety of budgerigars, canaries, cockatoos, parrots and rare British birds. Nearby was the locally named 'Sugar Basin', containing meteorological instruments.

By 1993 the Bird Aviary had become uneconomical and the council closed it down. The Aviary was a subject that brought a passionate response from people, both for and against. In the end, it was bulldozed at night! The 'Sugar Basin', managed by the Hudson Verity company, has been replaced by a fountain.

Nos 11–13 Brunswick Place, *c.*1930. The road runs from London Road to Dorset Street. In 1792 plans were drawn up for houses on the site, but they were not built until the 1820s owing to the war with France. The name comes from Caroline of Brunswick, wife of the Prince of Wales, later George IV.

The pleasant Georgian residential terrace was converted to offices and lodging houses during the 20th century and some properties suffered from bombing during World War Two. The above stretch was demolished in the 1970s and became business premises. The name Brunswick House, however, survives.

St Andrew's Presbyterian Church, on the corner of Brunswick Place and Dorset Street, was built in 1853 and was known as the 'Scotch Church'. It was chiefly founded by Andrew Lamb, a senior engineer of the P&O Shipping Line and could seat up to 700. Six hundred of the seats were reserved and paid for by members.

A Sunday School was also erected in 1884 by voluntary contributions, in memory of the founder. However, the Church eventually became redundant and was demolished in 1995. This modern and pleasant-looking Brunswick Gate office block, opposite the new Jurys Inn, was later built on the site.

East Park Terrace, directly facing Andrew's Park, was a genteel Victorian terrace that ran from New Road to Dorset Street. Several surgeons lived there and it also housed Miss Taylor's ladies' school, called 'Brownhills House', at No. 18. Miss Birch, a phrenologist, lived at No. 8!

Bomb damage and post-war development meant the complete destruction of the fine terrace, and it is currently home to an office block, an ambulance station and Southampton Solent University buildings. There are proposals for the offices and ambulance station to be replaced by a 21-storey, 204-bed hotel.

A view of Nos 59–63 St Andrew's Road in 1961. It was named after the nearby St Andrew's Presbyterian Church. The road led from Six Dials to the junction of Compton Walk and East Park Terrace. Much of it was destroyed during the Blitz and the site was used as allotments for many years.

The area was extensively developed during the late 1960s and early 1970s, when the Charlotte Place and Six Dials traffic schemes came into existence. This diverted the upper part of St Andrew's Road behind the old buildings, which were demolished and replaced by the above modern houses in the 1970s.

Clifford House incorporated various local government offices, including the vehicle taxation office, with Sparshatts Ltd Car Sales on the ground floor. The building in the background is the SPQR furniture showrooms, originally a Baptist Chapel but used as a Bible Christian Chapel from 1874 to 1934.

Clifford House was demolished and the 172-bed Premier Travel Inn, which also extends over the site of the former Sparshatts Car Sales parking area, was built on the site in 2002. The layout of the road junction, known as 'Six Dials' from its six converging roads, was drastically altered in the 1970s and 1980s.

Looking south down Exmouth Street from New Road, with a small bridge that led to Exmouth Place on the other side of the railway line. The houses date from the 1830s and were demolished in the late 1930s. Out of view, at No. 10 New Road on the right corner, was the Bay Tree Inn, damaged in the war and rebuilt in 1955.

The bridge over the railway has gone and the houses have been replaced by a car park. The road is now a cul-de-sac and on 13 February 1945 was the scene of an unsolved murder. Helen Hoyles, aged 55, a kitchen assistant at the American Red Cross in the High Street and a known prostitute, was found strangled here.

Taunton's School, rebuilt in New Road in 1878 to cater for 50 boys. The school was founded in 1760 to fit boys for a career at sea, by a bequest in the will of Alderman Richard Taunton. These premises were vacated in 1927 when the school, then a Grammar School with 431 pupils, moved to new premises in Highfield.

First-class education continues on the site, now occupied by the Southampton Solent University. Formerly the Southampton Institute, it was given university status in July 2005. It evolved from the College of Art, which was established in 1855, seven years before the Hartley Institute, now Southampton University.

Nos 25–23 Palmerston Road in 1935, and Nos 52–62 along North Front, on the right of the picture. These properties date back to the 1840s and this section of Palmerston Road was known as Portland Place in the 19th century. The ladies posing for the photographer seem to have a forerunner of the modern buggy.

The properties on the corner of Palmerston Road and North Front have now vanished, as has the entire north side of North Front. The large apartment block in the centre right is in New Road, and the opposite south side of the road was replaced by several blocks of modern flats and Kingsland House in the 1950s.

The south side of North Front in 1935, looking east from Palmerston Road towards St Mary Street and showing Nos 19–27. The houses were built in the 1840s and demolished in the late 1930s as part of a slum clearance programme. The spire of Holy Trinity Church, which served the Kingsland area, can be seen.

Moving further down North Front, we can now see Nos 15–19 and have moved closer to the church, with St Mary Street just visible in the distance. The church was completed in 1829 and was originally built as a chapel to the County Female Penitentiary. It was largely destroyed by bombing in World War Two.

A 1933 view of North Front, taken from the top of St Mary Street, with Nos 2–14 on the left. The rear of Nos 72–98 New Road is also shown on the right, bordering the Southern Railway main line leading to the Southampton West Station. The van is delivering milk by hand from a churn in the back.

Holy Trinity Church, which could seat 1,000 local worshippers, was destroyed in the Blitz of 1940 and the houses have been replaced by blocks of flats. Kingsway ring road was built across the district in the 1960s and lies immediately in front of the massive Premier Travel Inn that overlooks the area.

Nos 31–38 Winton Street, seen from St Mary Street in 1935, with Palmerston Park in the background. The street was recorded as Winchester Street in the 1820 St Mary's Church records. The name changed, to avoid conflict with another street of the same name, after Shirley came into the Borough in 1895.

Winton Street was demolished in the late 1930s and after World War Two much of the area was used for car parking for the nearby well-known Kingsland Market, now greatly reduced in size. It has only recently been redeveloped with modern housing, and the whole area has been given a new lease of life.

Craven Street ran from St Mary Street to Cossack Street, and this 1935 view shows the north side of the street, looking towards Cossack Street and Palmerston Park. It was part of a solid working-class district, one where the front doors were never locked because neighbours were trusted (and there was nothing to steal!).

Craven Street was demolished in the late 1930s as part of the area's slum clearance programme and, although some development took place in the 1960s, the current modern blocks of flats and small business premises have only been constructed in recent years.

The London Electric Wire Company, cable and wire manufacturers, occupies the corner site at 58 Ascupart Street, at the junction with Clifford Street. Next door is the Ascupart Infants School, built in 1882 to house 303 children. It was extended in March 1909 to accommodate the expanding local working-class population.

The corner premises and houses were demolished in 1960 as part of a clearance scheme, and the site now forms part of the further extended school premises. On the left is the 'Sure Start' centre that aims to help parents back into work by offering childcare and pre-school education.

Tom Fraser & Son's fine store occupied Nos 106–113 St Mary Street and was proudly advertised as 'Northam's leading draper, hardware dealer and paint merchant'. He also had wholesale drapers' premises in nearby Jail Street. His stout quality but cheap clothing was ideal for the working-class Chapel residents.

Out of town multiples, importing even cheaper mass-produced clothing and materials from abroad, brought an end to such stores as Fraser's. It is a sign of the times that the premises are now occupied by a number of small shops, including a betting shop and a Tesco Express self-service outlet.

The building adjoining the Kingsland Tavern at 76 St Mary Street was originally the public house's Tap Bar. A music hall occupied the upper floor in the early 19th century, and there were stables below. It also housed the town's first public library from 1889 until it moved to new premises in London Road in 1893.

This other 1983 view of St Mary Street also shows the Kingsland Tavern, run by the author's parents during the 1960s. The public house dates back to the early 1820s when the landlord was George Dean. Originally owned by the Hampton Court Brewery, it was taken over by Brickwood's in 1925 and Whitbread's in 1971.

The Clan Scotland Club building at 78 St Mary Street, on the corner of Johnson Street, was originally the Dorsetshire Arms, which dated back to the 1840s. Its address then was 8 Upper St Mary Street. The Exchange bookshop at No. 79 is next to the impressive sounding International Textiles premises at No. 80.

The Kingsland public house is unchanged, as is nearby Johnnie's Fisheries, but the Clan Scotland Club is now a sandwich bar; the Exchange Bookshop is the Just Add Music Shop and International Textiles is Forbes Dennehy, Funeral Directors, with newly-constructed accommodation above.

Looking west along South Front towards Above Bar in the 1950s. The Eagle Hotel can just be seen at the junction with Palmerston Road, adjoining the parks. The Robert Burns public house at 9 South Front, on the corner of Cossack Green, dates back to the 1860s and was shown as a beer house on the 1878 Drink Map.

Taken from further down the road, *c.*1965, the Adelaide Hotel at No. 10 South Front can also just be seen, as can the *News of the World* branch office at No. 17. The Eight Bells public house, on the corner of Broad Street, proudly displays that it is the headquarters of the Southampton Public Grounds Cricket Association.

The derelict remains of a tallow factory can be seen at the rear of South Front in the early 1960s. Tallow was solid animal fat obtained by heating and usually used for making candles, no doubt giving rise to bad smells! The 1899 directory shows Smith & Co., tallow chandlers, in occupation.

Extensive redevelopment has changed the scene dramatically, with a large block of modern flats replacing both the shops and public houses. The entrances of Broad Street and Cossack Green have now also vanished under the new buildings. The Eagle public house, renamed the Hogshead & Eagle in 1993, is all that remains.

In 1959 record dealer Henry's Band Box was on the corner of St Mary Street and James Street. On its left is what used to be the area's first Primitive Methodist Chapel, built in 1838. The Methodists moved to a new chapel in nearby South Front in 1887 and sold the St Mary Street building to the Oddfellows movement.

The Band Box building has now vanished completely, but the earlier chapel remains, now colourfully decorated by a pleasant wall painting. The Oddfellows sold the former chapel in 1966 and it became a betting shop, then the Mermaid Club, showing dubious films. It is now the City Centre Parish Office.

St Mary Street in 1935, showing William Fudge's hosiery at No. 27; R.W. Judd, newsagent at No. 28; Kellaway's hairdressers at No. 29; and the Jubilee Stores, Mr Metcalf's grocery shop, at No. 30. On the other corner of Chapel Street is No. 32, occupied by R. Hayter, a naturalist.

The shops changed into small-scale business premises during the post-war period and these, in turn, were later replaced by modern buildings. The remnants of Chapel Street are now bounded by the Southampton Information Technology Centre and a very recently constructed block of apartments.

This 1935 view of Cook Street, looking towards St Mary Street, shows Nos 3–8 on the south side of the street, shortly before they were demolished. They date back to the 1840s and the terraced houses were basic, with an outside toilet in a small rear garden. However, they were better than the slums in the town centre.

Post-war development took place in this area and the pleasant apartment block, which has now replaced the terraced houses, is Southampton Solent University's Hamwic Hall of Residence, named after the original eighth-century Anglo-Saxon town. There is now a clear view of the unchanged block at the end of the road.

The lower end of St Mary Street, opposite St Mary's Church, in 1941. No. 20, on the extreme left, had been occupied in 1940 by Charles Wilkins, poultry dealer; No. 21 by Alfred Walker, leather goods; No. 22 by Lewis, tobacconists; and No. 24 by Harris, chemists. They were demolished soon after the photograph was taken.

This part of St Mary Street, where it used to curve to meet East Street to its left, was known as Bag Row in ancient times, probably from Richard Bagg, a 14th-century local landowner. The shops have been replaced by pleasant housing and small business premises.

The west side of lower St Mary Street, between the junctions with East Street to the left and Cook Street to the right. The Premium Trading Stamp Company proudly boasts that it has 'branches everywhere' and Herbert James Holt, ironmonger, has an amazing display of wares outside his extensive premises.

Most of the shops, including the Green Man Inn at the extreme right of the earlier photograph, were destroyed in the 1940 Blitz, but the modern apartments were built only recently. Surprisingly, although the public house licence was suspended, it was not surrendered by Brickwood's Brewery until August 1970.

This early 1900s photograph is faded but interesting, because it shows the costermongers who used to set up their handcarts, selling anything from fruit and vegetables to pots and pans, along the wall of the Deanery. On the extreme right is Southampton's first drinking fountain, erected at the bottom of East Street in 1856.

The eastern area of the Deanery was replaced by the Methodist Central Hall in 1925. It was sold to the City Council in 1965 and is now an active Community Church. St Mary's Church, in the background, is the town's mother church, from Saxon times, and was re-erected in 1879–84. The spire was completed in 1914.

Edwin Jones came to Southampton from Romsey in 1860 and opened a small drapery shop in East Street. It soon developed into this imposing late Victorian department store, seen here fronting Hoglands Park and viewed from Palmerston Road. Edwin, who held strong religious and humanitarian views, died in 1896.

The west section of the former Victorian store, also known as Queen's Buildings, has been replaced by the modern dual carriage Queens Way ring road. Other large stores have also been constructed at the bottom of Hanover Buildings and the area remains a focal point for local shoppers.

The East Street frontage of Edwin Jones & Co. Ltd in 1930 and the site of the first Edwin Jones haberdashery shop, which he rented with his two sisters in the 1860s. An astute businessman, who made his initial capital by dealing in cotton during the American Civil War, Edwin was twice Mayor of Southampton.

Edwin Jones & Co. Ltd later became part of the Drapery Trust and in 1928 was absorbed by the Debenhams Group and extensively modernised. However, the store name was not changed until 1973. It was virtually destroyed in the 1940 Blitz and completely rebuilt in the late 1950s.

A post-war view of lower East Street, with the Edwin Jones store on the left. Bollom Dry Cleaners is on the corner with Orchard Lane and Granville Stores and F.W. Woolworth's are on the right. East Street then ran right down to Marsh Lane, where the Methodist Central Hall can be seen in the background.

Edwin Jones's store is now called Debenhams and a 'bargain' shop, selling a wide variety of cheap goods, has taken over the Granville and Woolworth stores. The East Street Centre now blocks East Street and the view of the Central Hall. On the left is the external fire exit of the large Capital House office block.

The town centre was shattered in the early years of World War Two, when the Luftwaffe tried to take the heart out of Southampton. This 1941 view of lower East Street is typical of the result, but the cycles parked outside the damaged butchers, E.A. Chard, show that some remnants of normality continued to exist.

The large store of Edwin Jones, next to Chard the butchers, recovered from the Blitz and was redeveloped in 1957 and enlarged to include the sites of the former adjacent premises. East Street was completely rebuilt and Debenhams remains one of the principal and most popular stores in the city.

Another view of the shattered Edwin Jones department store and E.A. Chard, butchers, this time taken from Orchard Lane. These scenes were a familiar sight to the author in his childhood and playing on such bombed sites allowed us the freedom to indulge in further damage without the risk of getting a modern ASBO!

Extensive post-war redevelopment has meant there is now no trace of the former destruction. Small business premises, shops and restaurants have replaced the ruins, the Edwin Jones store has been rebuilt and the modern motor car now swamps the town centre, in spite of ever-increasing parking charges.

Victor Value, East Street, 1961. This was a London-based supermarket group, owned by Alex Cohen, operating at the lower end of the grocery trade in the 1960s. Although no relation to Jack Cohen, the founder of Tesco, Alex Cohen sold Victor Value to Tesco in 1968 for £8.4 million.

Victor Value was known as VV, as the handles on the doors of the store read 'VV' when shut. Tesco converted the larger branches to its own brand and sold the smaller units. This photograph was taken from a different angle to show the large block of 18 apartments and retail units under construction in East Street.

Looking north along East Street, towards High Street, in 1962. One can see, from left to right: Vincent Gargaro, fruiterer; the Snack Bar, light refreshments; Barnes, paints and wallpaper; Garret & Haysom, monumental, marble/stone masons; and Maxwell, clothing, all prior to the entrance of Back-of-the-Walls.

East Street is no longer two-way and now has extensive parking on both sides of the road. All the shop premises have changed hands, including the former boarded-up premises on the far corner with Back-of-the-Walls, and there is no longer a monumental stone mason in the area.

Looking along Nos 39–52 Lime Street in 1935, towards the junction with Queen Street, seen in the background. Originally called The Rookery on one side, then Cross Street, the street became Lime Street in around 1900. 'Coleman's Blue' was a popular small bag placed in the rinse to make washing appear whiter.

Slum clearance in the 1930s resulted in what were then modern blocks of flats replacing the Gospel Mission Hall on the right, but post-war redevelopment, following extensive bomb damage, altered the area beyond recognition. The popular and long-standing Godwin's fish and chip shop continues, under new ownership.

Bell Street dates back to at least 1813, and this 1935 view looks east from the Canal Walk end to Orchard Lane, seen in the distance. The junction with Cross Street is in the right foreground. The children posing for the photograph, although in a poor neighbourhood, appear clean and properly dressed.

This is all that now remains of the truncated Bell Street, with the block of Orchard Lane flats on the corner of Lime Street in the background. Cross Street was demolished in the 1930s. The flats on the right were built in the 1950s and the low building on the left is that of 'Fairbridge', a youth development organisation.

Orchard Lane in 1935, with East Street in the background. Nos 1–6 Orchard Lane are between East Street (at the far left of the picture) and Lime Street. The original Godwin's fish and chip shop is on the corner at No. 7, the Home Away from Home refreshment rooms are at Nos 9–10 and Hamer, tailors, is at No. 11.

All the buildings were swept away in the slum clearances of the 1930s and replaced by what were then modern blocks of flats. East Street is just beyond the large van, parked near the entrance of the small Orchard Lane Evangelical-cum-Baptist church, built in the 1970s on the corner of Lime Street.

W.J. Axton, at Nos 16–19 Orchard Lane, dealt in ship machinery and was also a general store. Next door, at No. 20, was Bertram Robert Dunford's fish and chip saloon, adjoining the delightfully named Charlie's Court, although the origin of the name is unknown. Finally, at No. 21, is Bahsh Poswell, draper.

The Burton Tavern, at 26 Orchard Lane, used to be known as the Burton Ale House. It held a beer licence before 1869 and changed its name in the 1890s. Owned by Winchester's Welch's Hyde Abbey Brewery in the early 20th century, it was a Watney's house when its licence was finally surrendered in April 1957.

The Diamond Jubilee Inn at 65 Orchard Lane was named to commemorate Queen Victoria's Jubilee in 1897, but it was a beer house before that, dating back to the early 1860s. Next door, at No. 67, is F. Tong, basket maker, and at No. 68 is Riggs Leather Stores. These premises are between Mount Street and Bell Street.

The earlier Orchard Lane photographs were taken c.1956, just prior to their demolition as part of the extensive development of the area. This 2007 view, looking towards East Street, shows just how dramatically the area has changed in character, with large blocks of flats replacing the small terraced shops.

Ocean Trading (Wholesale) Ltd, at 40 Orchard Lane, next door to the Lounge Bar of the Globe Hotel, was a fancy goods dealer on the corner of Bernard Street, opposite the entrance of Oxford Street. At Nos 37 and 38 on the far left, on the corner of College Street, is the grocery shop of Francis Blake.

The Globe Hotel, a listed building, was due to be restored in 1991 and turned into a trendy bar called Harry Lime's. Local objections to its application for a music and dancing licence succeeded and it became an apartment block instead. Orchard Lane has been realigned some distance from this original position.

The Russell Tavern, in 1956, at the junction of Russell Street and King Street, under the management of Mr Albert Edward Norman. It dated back to the early 1850s, when it was known as the Ship Inn. The name changed in the early 1890s, when Marstons Brewery took over the property from the Winchester Brewery.

The Russell Tavern was demolished shortly after the earlier photograph was taken, and this four-storey block of council flats, called Marsh House, was built on the site. Behind it is a similar block, called All Saints House. King Street is now a cul-de-sac and no longer runs into East Street.

Nos 68–72 Bernard Street in 1956, with what were then very familiar names in the town. Frederick Misselbrook and Arthur Weston founded their chain of retail grocery outlets in 1848 and were among the first to introduce 'cash and carry' wholesale trading. J. Jeski & Sons specialised in goods for ships' crew.

More familiar local names. Collis & Co., at Nos 78–80, were wholesale tobacconists who boasted they were 'wholesalers of the south' with branches in Portsmouth, Ryde and Worthing. The adjoining Bailey & Co. were builders of some standing, but the street's underground toilets in front were of ill-repute!

Although of poor quality, the author was delighted to discover this photograph of 111 Bernard Street, where he was born. It is on the left of No. 109, on the right corner with Latimer Street. This photograph was taken in the 1930s and the terrace is typical of the street. Much of this area is owned by Queen's College, Oxford.

The premises on the north side of Bernard Street were demolished in the late 1950s and replaced by the St Bernard House block of flats and St James Church, now the St Nicholas Greek Orthodox Church. Nos 109–111 Bernard Street, seen on the far right, have been rebuilt and upper Latimer Street is now a precinct.

The Glasgow Hotel stood on the corner of Bernard Street and Orchard Place, on the site of an 1840s hotel originally called Pullinger's, later the Clarendon. It boasted it had hot, cold and vapour baths and that the owner spoke French! It became the Glasgow Hotel in the 1880s and was owned by Cooper's Brewery.

The hotel, known as the Glasgow Restaurant and Oyster Grotto in 1925, was destroyed in the Blitz of 1940. Replaced by a temporary shack and again called the Glasgow Hotel, it was rebuilt in 1958. It was refurbished in September 1990 and reopened as Dixies, but is now the offices of Martin's Rubber Co. Ltd.

An early view of Oxford Street, looking east towards Terminus Terrace with the Terminus Railway Station visible at the end of the road. This was built in 1839 for the London & South Western Railway at a cost of £10,500. On the right-hand corner of Latimer Street is John Adams, export bookseller and stationer.

The Terminus Station building no longer serves the railway, the station having closed to passengers in 1966, and it is now the Stanley Casino. The John Adams bookshop has become the Poppadom Express Restaurant and Bar and the former Oxford Temperance Hotel, on the left, is now the White Star restaurant.

Oxford Street, facing Bernard Street. On the right, on the corner of John Street, is the Oxford public house, owned by Forder's Hampton Court Brewery, easily confused with the Oxford Temperance Hotel further down on the corner of Latimer Street. The Grapes public house on the left dates back to the early 1850s.

Other than the Grapes public house, all the businesses have changed considerably. The popular and well-known Kuti's Brasserie, famous locally for its curries, is now on the left, near the Grapes pub. The Oxford public house is now the Oxford Brasserie and on the opposite corner of John Street is Pizza Express.

A post-war view of Oxford Street, at the junction with Bernard Street and Orchard Place, with Goldsmith & Clark's newsagents and tobacconists on the right corner. Next door is U. Micklethwaite, potato merchant, then Hooper's Temperence Hotel and Fred Trim Ltd, wholesale fruit, banana and potato merchants.

The terrace has undergone changes, with the potato merchant and hotel replaced by an office block and private accommodation. The Sailors' Home, erected in 1910 at a cost of £10,000, is in the far distance. Now the Salvation Army 'Mountbatten Centre', it is undergoing redevelopment and is seen here without a roof.

This *c.*1920 view shows the York & Albany public house at the junction of the lower end of Albert Road (curving away to the left) with Lower Bridge Road. It had a beer licence before 1869 and served the local dock workers living in the area. The billboards are advertising *Chicago* at the King's Theatre, Southsea.

Lower Bridge Road was swept away during the construction of the Itchen Bridge (which opened in 1977), and the steps on the right give access to the roundabout where the Itchen Bridge joins Central Bridge. The extreme edge of the Grade II listed Royal Albert Hotel, at 123 Albert Road, can just be seen on the left.

Nelson Street, linking Chapel Road and Anglesea Terrace, Northam, in 1965. It is not shown on the 1842 map but appears on the 1845 town map. The author's grandparents lived nearby, in the adjacent Paget Street, and he remembers how their front door gave immediate entry to the prized 'front room'.

This 2007 photograph is taken from the opposite end of Nelson Street as entry is not possible to the former area, which is a secured building site. However, the above photograph serves to show how Nelson Street is being transformed into blocks of apartments that the author's grandparents would not recognise.

Chapel Road, an ancient road that was part of the grid pattern of streets in the Saxon town of Hamwic, linked nearby St Mary's Church with the Chapel Mill and shore of the River Itchen. Nos 11 and 12, on the corner of Grove Street, were occupied by Riley & Davies Ltd, wholesale tobacconists and confectioners.

This section of Chapel Road's pre-1842 houses, here photographed c.1965, was on the south side of the road, with the junction with Paget Street (where the author's grandparents lived) on the far right. No. 46 was Barrow's General Store, managed by Reginald Herbert, next door to Arthur Lawe's grocery shop at No. 47.

This part of Chapel Road is also on the south side, at the junction with Nelson Street. The footbridge of the railway level crossing can just be seen on the far right. No. 57 was Miss G. Finn's greengrocers, with Ernest Chard's butchers and Renaldo Spacagna's boot repairers on opposite corners.

All the houses in Chapel Road were demolished in the late 1960s and the cleared space was used for parking for some years. However, industrial units have since been built on this south side, ahead of the junction with Paget Street, and new large apartment blocks are now along the length of both Paget and Nelson Streets.

The south side of Anglesea Terrace, *c.*1965, taken from the junction with Glebe Road, with No. 1 Glebe Road on the right corner. It was built before 1842 and housed good, solid working-class families, many of whom were dock workers. In the background is the Eastern District School, with a roof playground, for 935 pupils.

The houses were demolished shortly after the earlier photograph was taken, and the area was used for many years as a lorry park for heavy goods vehicles. These newly constructed duplex apartments, with their underground car parking facilities, have now made this part of Southampton a desirable area to live in.

Nos 1–5 Anglesea Terrace, Chapel, *c.*1965. No. 3 was occupied in the 1940s by Patrick Risden and his family at a weekly rent of 12s 6d. The house had a front bedroom, two linked bedrooms at the rear, a living room and a front room that was rarely used. There was a scullery, outside toilet and a spotless black-leaded stove.

It should be added that, in common with other houses in the area, the key to the front door was kept on a piece of string accessed via the letter box! The pre-1842 houses were demolished in the late 1960s and the adjacent Anglesea Tavern public house, on the corner of Albert Road, is now called the Chapel Arms.

These houses, *c.*1964, are in Albert Road, just north of the junction with Elm Terrace on the right. The road was constructed in 1837 by the Itchen Bridge Company to link the Chapel area with the newly constructed floating bridge. It was originally called Floating Bridge Road and it was a working-class district.

The houses were demolished in the late 1960s and the district was further transformed when the nearby Itchen Bridge was constructed in 1977 to replace the floating bridges across the River Itchen. The City Council Refuse Depot, the main household waste recycling centre, now occupies the site.

This 1930 photograph shows the Jubilee Inn on the corner of Belvidere Road and Victoria Street, with the Northam gas holder in the background. The inn had a beer licence before 1869 and is shown on the town's 1878 Drink Map. It was originally owned by Barlow's Victoria Brewery, but it later belonged to Brickwoods.

The Jubilee Inn was not given a full licence until March 1960, but it closed in July 1974 when its licence lapsed. The building became an office for some time, then a café until after 1995. It was subsequently demolished for these car showrooms and garage when the area was further developed for light industry.

Nos 68–56 Millbank Street, Northam, *c.*1956, showing houses on the east side of the street south of the junction with William Street. They were probably built in the 1870s to house the ever-growing local working-class population, many of whom worked in the nearby shipyards on the bank of the River Itchen.

The houses were demolished in the late 1950s and light industrial units were built on the site. These currently include Tile World, the Fireplaces UK Heating Centre and Anthony Forfar Interiors. The shipyards no longer exist as such, but are instead used as a yacht marina with associated shops and facilities.

Britannia Road at the junction with Guildford Street, Northam, in 1960. The Southampton Co-operative Society warehouse is on the extreme left and the pleasant houses are, from left to right: Magdala, Cathcart, Trouville and Carisbrook. They were all demolished as part of the Northam No. 4 Clearance Scheme in 1960.

Only the Co-operative Society building now remains, although the society no longer owns it. The fine houses have been swept away and replaced by a car sales forecourt. This area has changed in character considerably since the St Mary's Football Stadium was built further down the road.

Northam Railway Station was opened on 1 September 1872 as a result of popular demand from the local inhabitants, and was constructed by local builders J. Bull & Sons, who were involved with many similar stations in the area. The Northam Road latticed metal bridge over the line was reconstructed in 1908.

The station eventually fell into disuse in the 1960s and was left to decay after it closed in 1966. Both platforms were removed in 1969 and it became derelict. However, this changed dramatically when the St Mary's football stadium was built nearby and this new access was created for the fans and locals.

Northam Road in 1959, taken from the mouth of Augustine Road and showing the opposite junction with Kent Street on the left. The corner bakery is that of G. Martin and to its right are the boarded-up premises of Harley of Northam, adjacent to T. Craddock, hairdresser, Kelly, butchers and the Northam Inn.

The entire terrace, opposite the Northam Social Club, was demolished in 1960 and a petrol filling station built on the site of the shops and public house. New building work is currently taking place beyond the filling station. The Northam Inn dated back to the 1850s, when it was known as the New Inn.

These mid-Victorian houses in Campbell Street, Northam, are pictured in 1970, shortly before they were demolished as part of a clearance scheme. Many of the residents originated from either the Caribbean or India, settling in Southampton during the 1950s and 1960s.

A children's play area now occupies the site, but it appears to be under-utilised, as although many of the former residents still live in the district their children are now much older. The Plaza cinema, formerly next to the site, was replaced by a TV broadcasting organisation. It is now empty and awaiting development.

A view of the very popular Plaza Cinema in December 1957, shortly after it closed on 30 November. Opened in 1932, it had seating for 2,100 and the opening film was *Looking on the Bright Side* starring Gracie Fields. The back row double seats, used by courting couples, are a well-remembered feature!

It is ironic that the building was taken over by a TV company, the very reason for the decline in cinema audiences. The premises were used by Southern Television, which went on air in 1958, but the buildings were eventually replaced. It is now empty as Meridian TV, who replaced STV in 1993, left in 2004.

Nos 200–208 Northam Road, on the east side, just north of the junction with Princes Street, *c.*1956. This terrace was built in the 1840s on the approach to the Northam Bridge, built in 1799. Mr Servergnini's Plaza Snack Bar at No. 200 is named after the cinema that was built on the opposite side of the road in 1932.

The houses were demolished soon after the earlier photograph was taken, and a large suite of modern offices was later built on the site. Traffic lights, protected by a camera, have been installed on this busy junction that covers the main east–west city traffic across Northam Bridge.

Northam Road toll bridge, *c*.1920, with the closed gates of the entrance to the rebuilt 1889 wrought-iron Northam Bridge in the background. The Welcome Home public house is on the corner of Summer Street, on the left, and Barlow's Brewery Ship Inn, which dates back to the 1830s, is further down on the right.

This end of Northam Road is now a cul-de-sac leading to the bank of the River Itchen. It was created in 1954 when the new Northam Bridge, one of the first in the country made from pre-stressed concrete, was opened. The Welcome Home was demolished in the 1930s when the nearby Plaza Cinema was built.

Looking north along MacNaghten Road in 1905, towards Harcourt Road. Built in the 1890s by the National Liberal Land Company as part of the new Bitterne Park Estate, it was named after Sir Steuart MacNaghten (1815–1895) who lived at Bitterne Manor House. He was knighted in 1890 by Queen Victoria.

The Wheatsheaf Wine & Spirit Stores has been converted into a modern block of flats, and modern housing has replaced the former shop premises and private dwellings. Parked cars are now a feature of the street where once children happily played without fear of traffic.

The launching of the *Alberta II*, built by Ted Dyer and christened by his sister Dorrie at Dyer's Boatyard, Cobden Bridge, on 22 September 1933. Jean Underhill is the baby in the arms of her mother, Mrs Lillian Walker, and the second lady from the left is her sister Olive, who worked in service for the Dyers for 11 years.

Son Terry Dyer still runs the popular boatyard that is well known to the local boating fraternity. The 1883 Cobden Bridge was rebuilt and opened in 1928 at a cost of £45,000, and the landmark Bitterne Park Triangle Clock Tower, moved here in 1934–35, is now just visible on the Bitterne Park side of the bridge.

All Hallows Church, at the junction of Wakefield Road and Witts Hill, Midanbury. It was built in 1951 as the daughter church of the Anglican Church of the Ascension in Cobden Avenue, when the parish boundary, previously at Midanbury, moved east towards Bitterne and northwards towards Townhill Park.

The earlier photograph, taken in May 1959, shows a separate bell tower outside the simple but pleasant looking church that is linked with Naminage Parish, Uganda. The tower was incorporated into the main building when the church was enlarged in 1965 to cater for the needs of the expanding nearby estate.

Henry W. Rowles's garage and Esso service station, 165 Bitterne Road, at the junction with Cobbett Road in October 1960. Further down, to its left, next to Benjamin Mark's chemists with the mock Tudor front, is part of the Fairways Motors garage, showrooms, self-drive, accessories and offices complex.

The junction is now controlled by traffic lights, and Bitterne Road is a dual carriageway, 'protected' by speed and other monitoring cameras. The outside petrol pumps are a thing of the past and the former H.W. Rowles garage now only deals with replacement tyres, exhausts, batteries and brakes.

Lance's Hill, Bitterne, *c.*1915, looking west towards the town and showing a pleasant, rural and leisurely scene. Originally called Great Lance's Hill, after David Lance who built Chessel House in 1797, this road bordered his estate on its north side. He was the main instigator of the construction of Northam Bridge.

The construction of the Bitterne by-pass in the early 1980s means that this stretch of what is now a dual carriageway is open to westbound traffic and eastbound buses and taxis. The junction with Maybray King Way, which skirts the former Bitterne Village and is open to two-way traffic, is located at the traffic lights.

Mrs Guy's shop in Bitterne Road, *c.*1935, opposite the Red Lion public house. It was one of the many thatched cottages with cob walls to be found in Bitterne in the 19th century. Close to the old Bitterne School it thus became the local 'tuck shop'. To its right are Hornby's Bitterne Dairy and Boyes Bakery.

Mrs Guy's shop was demolished when Bitterne Parade, a thriving parade of small shops, was built shortly after the earlier photograph was taken. This was recently completely refurbished and Savers, at the end of the parade, is now on the cottage site. The former dairy is now Hayton's florists.

Bitterne Road, *c.*1982, looking west towards Lances Hill, immediately prior to the construction of the by-pass. To the right is the United Reformed Church (formerly the Congregational Chapel) on the corner of Chapel Street. It was built in 1897 and demolished in 1983 as part of the redevelopment.

Bitterne Road has changed dramatically and this section is now an underpass. It is not possible to take a photograph from the same position as the above photograph. The Red Lion Hotel is now visible because the former row of shops has been demolished. The United Reformed Church was relocated in the new precinct.

Nos 1–13 Maytree Road, Bitterne, *c*.1968. This road appears on the 1881 map unnamed and with only a few houses. The first stretch of houses, called Bitterne Terrace, was on the opposite, west side, of the road. In the background is the Bitterne Bowl, built on the site of the Ritz Cinema, which closed in July 1961.

The name Maytree Road is preserved as the walkway to Bitterne Precinct from the southern section of Angel Crescent (named after the Angel Inn that was demolished to extend the Sainsbury's store). The houses were razed to create part of Angel Crescent and this car park that serves Sainsbury's and local shops.

The Elephant & Castle, Bursledon Road, in 2003. It was a popular public house, erected in the 1930s and extended and modernised in 1966. It was built on the site of an 1860s public house, nicknamed the Old Black House because it had corrugated iron walls and a black tarpaulin roof.

Plans for development of the site were announced in 2003 and there were demonstrations against it, but these were in vain as it was razed in September 2005. This view is taken from a different angle to show the 15 flats and 19 terraced houses built on the former site and car park. Ten flats were also built in its garden.

There had been a post office at the junction of North East Road and South East Road since the late 1880s, when Miss Mary Kersley was the sub-postmistress. In early 1900 it was called 'The People's Supply Stores', selling a wide range of products. It was an essential service for the local community, especially pensioners.

The post office succumbed to the pressures and financial demands of corporate management, like so many others in the area, and closed in 2007. The former shop premises were extended at the rear, with parking space provided, and converted into four apartments.

Derelict and neglected waste ground at the junction of South East Road and Kathleen Road in February 1937. Top centre, on the corner, advertising Hovis and 'Quality Confectionery', is the Bay Bakery. On the opposite corner is Harold Bennett's grocery shop – the junction is called 'Bennett's Corner' to this day.

The new Sholing Village Green, on 22 April 2007, opened by John Denham MP. The Bay Bakery is now housing and Bennett's grocery shop is a hairdressers. The green has been fenced, returfed, trees planted and benches erected, all supported by the Sholing Environment Group, City Council and Countryside Agency.

James Wiffen ran his grocery and confectionery shop, known as Castle Stores, on the corner of Station Road and Spring Road, Sholing, for many years. This photograph was taken in around 1950. The Classic Cinema poster on the wall is advertising the films *Return of the Bad Men* and *Comanche Territory*.

The corner shop, so much a part of normal life, is now a disappearing resource, having succumbed to the commercial dominance of the large multiple stores that now inhabit the town. This shop has been converted and enlarged for residential use.

Lankester & Crook Ltd, on the south-west side of Station Road, at the junction with Portsmouth Road, was not only a general store, bakers and butchers; it was also a much-used post office. Behind the butchers shop was their large Alexandra Bakery, producing enough loaves and confectionery to serve the entire district.

Although the buildings have not changed dramatically, their use certainly has. The Lankester & Crook complex is long gone and has been replaced by a colourful 'Pete's Place Pizza'; Hussey Construction Ltd; Scizzorz unisex hairdressers; Scott's Barber Shop; and the Sholing Cycle Centre.

The junction of Manor Road, Woolston *c.*1941, not far from Radstock Road, with Drummond Road leading off to the right. The empty corner building at 9a Manor Road had been a cycle shop. This is a good example of the devastating effect of bomb blast, as none of the houses in the photograph suffered a direct hit.

Drummond Road no longer exists and all the houses and the corner shop in the previous picture have been demolished. This area is now called Norton Close. The junction with Radstock Road is just visible on the left and the path on the right leads to housing in Swanage Close, on the site of the former Drummond Road.

The northern end of Manor Road, near the junction with Sholing Road in 1941, showing the extent of bomb blast damage to Nos 214–230. Manor Road existed before 1900 but with only a few scattered houses. These properties were built in the early 1930s, around the same time as the adjoining Merry Oak estate.

The damage was clearly so severe that the houses had to be completely rebuilt, and they now have a more modern appearance. This scene was repeated throughout Southampton, where 1,848 properties were completely destroyed, 5,214 damaged beyond repair and 17,060 badly damaged but repairable.

Lankester & Crook Ltd in Obelisk Road, Woolston, were popular grocers, wine and spirit merchants, butchers, bakers and ironmongers. They had branches in Victoria Road, Portsmouth Road, Station Road, Bitterne Road, Manor Farm Road, Portswood Road, Shirley Road, Hedge End, Netley and Chandlers Ford.

The private paraffin pump has vanished and Lankester & Crook Ltd, which was formed in 1901, sold their business and properties to a property and maintenance company in 1986. Part of the building is empty and the remainder is occupied by a cycle shop, hairdressers, shoe/clothing shop and a dance centre.

The first fire station serving Woolston was established in 1896 in Weston Grove Road and manned by the St Mary Extra Brigade, with two officers and five men. This station was built in Portsmouth Road, at a cost of £9,471, and opened in October 1929. It also initially housed a Guy ambulance, operated by the Brigade.

The Fire Station closed in January 1996, when the appliances and personnel moved to a new Fire Station in Bursledon Road, Hightown. Refurbished, the building is now the very popular Old Fire Station Surgery, an NHS Group Practice covering Woolston, Sholing, Netley, Bursledon and Hamble.

The lower end of Bridge Road, Woolston, in 1910, at the junction with Portsmouth Road. The railway bridge leading to Woolston Railway Station is in the background and Oakbank Road is on the left. The horse trough, removed in the late 1950s, was donated by voluntary subscriptions in 1902.

The attractive, and so far un-vandalised Millennium Garden and car park have replaced the former offices and shops, and the railway bridge can just be glimpsed underneath the 1977 Itchen Bridge. The Millennium Garden has a 10-metre high feather sculpture made of stainless steel and recycled glass.

The Southern Gas Board showroom on the corner of Bridge Road and Portsmouth Road, Woolston, was a familiar sight for many years and their range of cookers was always on display outside their premises. Directly opposite, in Bridge Road on the left, is the shop of William Parker, tobacconist.

The former Gas Board premises are now occupied by the Motor World car accessories shop and the telephone kiosk has been removed. The opposite shop premises in Bridge Road were demolished when the Itchen Bridge was constructed in 1977 and the site is now a public car park.

The corner of Bridge Road and Portsmouth Road, Woolston, was occupied by solicitors Bell, Pope and Bridgewater until it was destroyed in World War Two. The popular Coliseum Coaches Company later set up a temporary building on the site as a local sales room. A milk vending machine can be seen to its right.

The temporary building still remains but is no longer in use, and alongside is the Woolston Millennium Garden. The 'feather' sculpture represents part of its central theme of flight and float, with the garden around it divided into three segments by a propeller-shaped brick path, representing land, sea and sky.

Looking west down Portsmouth Road from the junction with Victoria Road, Woolston, towards the River Itchen, *c.*1900. One of the floating bridges can be seen mid-stream. The first floating bridge crossed the river in November 1836 and its first cash customer was the 'Red Rover' stagecoach on its way to Bristol.

The river view and the west Southampton shoreline are now obscured by modern housing and a span of the massive Itchen Bridge that replaced the floating bridges in 1977. The housing block has also replaced the Woolston Coffee & Refreshment Rooms at the river's edge and traffic lights now control the junction.

This 1937 aerial view shows the early Supermarine Works, founded in 1913 by Noel Pemberton-Billing and Hubert Scott-Paine. Their 'flying lifeboats', launched from the concrete ramp, developed into several famous classes of military and civilian amphibians, many of them winning the famous Schneider Trophy.

The factory later produced the famous Spitfire fighter, developed by R.J. Mitchell, but was destroyed in 1940 by the Luftwaffe. The aerial view cannot be accurately reproduced, but this photograph, taken from the high-level 1977 Itchen Bridge, serves to show the dramatic changes, with only the concrete ramp surviving.

A nostalgic 1977 view of one of the last floating bridges, seen crossing the River Itchen from the town side. They were an essential part of the transport system, connecting with the Corporation bus link at Woolston, vehicles in Portsmouth Road and carrying workers for the large Vosper Thornycroft ship-building complex.

The floating bridges were removed when the Itchen Bridge was opened, soon after the earlier photograph was taken, and attractive housing was later built on the former bus link site. Vosper Thornycroft, started by John I. Thornycroft in 1904, relocated to Portsmouth in 2004, and the site is currently awaiting development.

On the left of the coal barges is Southampton's first Outer Dock, completed in 1842 and renamed Princess Alexandra Dock in 1967. It was then a roll-on roll-off terminal. The link-span, just beyond the barges, was built at 6 Berth for the Norwegian Thoresons car ferry service that commenced operations in 1964.

The car ferry service withdrew in 1984 and other extensive dock developments meant that the original dock was no longer needed. A joint venture company then developed the 75-acre site into what is now called 'Ocean Village', with its complex of shops, offices, apartments and a large secure marina.

A view from the newly constructed Itchen Bridge in the late 1970s, with Canute Road in the background, at the junction with Floating Bridge Road and the Old Docks. The Marsh Hotel, 42 Canute Road, is at the extreme right of the picture. It dates back to at least 1878 and became a Marstons Brewery house in 1957.

The Marsh Hotel is now private accommodation and Floating Bridge Road has become a redeveloped small truncated section, serving several small industrial units. The former section of the Old Docks is now part of the extensive 'Ocean Village' complex, with large blocks of luxury apartments.

This derelict shelter in Floating Bridge Road, on the Chapel side of the River Itchen, was used to protect passengers waiting for the Corporation buses or floating bridges. It is here awaiting demolition prior to the construction of the Itchen Bridge. The pram could not be taken on board a modern bus!

The former shelter is now the site of one of the massive supporting pillars of the Itchen Bridge and a boatyard. Nearby is the City Council's Southampton Water Activities Centre, where youngsters are taught canoeing and water skills. Only a cul-de-sac section of Floating Bridge Road now remains, with no housing.

INDEX

ND - #0361 - 270225 - C0 - 260/197/12 - PB - 9781780913278 - Gloss Lamination